AN EYE FOR BIRDS

An Eye for Birds

Reflections on Nature and Conservation

Bruce Kendrick

Whittles Publishing

Whittles Publishing Ltd.,
Dunbeath,
Caithness, KW6 6EG,
Scotland, UK

www.whittlespublishing.com

Printed in the UK by Short Run Press, Exeter

To my wonderful Ma, Dot

CONTENTS

Acknowledgements

I'm glad you took time out to read this page as I owe a huge debt to five fine individuals. Without their help this book would still be a semi-structured autobiographical narrative of a young man's love of nature and some musings through the lens of his old age.

The first of these is a good friend, Cynan Jones, who is a top published fiction writer. You see, I had been lured into a shabby publishing deal by one of these 'vanity' publishing scams; I was seeking Cynan's advice. He told me to stay well clear of these rip-off merchants. I think he was managing my disappointment when he suggested I send him the manuscript. I gratefully complied and after two weeks he phoned and suggested we have lunch. We met in one of our favourite spots, near his home in Aberaeron, on the Cardigan Bay coast. Several risotto lunches and more than eighteen months later, we had a manuscript ready for a publisher's gaze. "Be prepared for push backs" was Cynan's straight advice. Cynan's support, as my good friend and mentor throughout this time, means so much to me.

It was my second piece of good fortune when Keith Whittles emailed me to say he would like to publish the text. Whittles had been recommended to me by another good friend, Mike Crutch from Morayshire. One of his pals, also published by them, passed on his view that they are a top company and a pleasure to deal with. He was so right.

The next slice of good fortune was when Keith Whittles chose Caroline Petherick to edit my debut manuscript. Not only has Caroline done a superb technical job but I do believe she has added, with her gentle guidance, much more to that original script. It helps that she believes in the world of nature conservation and evolution as much as I do.

My final thank you has to go to my wife and partner, Lynn. She gave, and continues to give, her time and support, so that I can try to make a decent fist of this writing malarky.

Bruce Kendrick

INTRODUCTION

The slower drive from Crickhowell to Cowbridge, over the Black Mountains in the Brecon Beacons National Park, takes a scenic single-track road. It climbs to the private Glanusk shooting estate, owned by the Legge-Bourke family, and passes through it.

Here in 2013, with a search warrant issued by the Dyfed-Powys Police, the RSPB collected hard evidence of one of the largest mass raptor poisonings on recent record. Fresh carcasses of seven dead red kites and three common buzzards were found hidden in sacks near a pheasant pen on the Glanusk estate and belonging to it.[1] While this evidence is of course only circumstantial, Dyfed-Powys Police have not yet brought any prosecutions. Naturally, a few suspect the royal connection is at play; the establishment looking after its own, not dissimilar to the much-reported incident of Prince Harry and two dead hen harriers at Sandringham in 2007.[2] As with many such raptor killings on grouse moors or shooting estates, top legal teams and PR agencies are employed, some say to obfuscate and prevaricate with sublime sophistry. Plato called them out when he described sophists as 'sham philosophers'.

The peaceful Usk Valley, with its country estates, superb fishing, abundant bird life and top-notch hotels, is left behind as the narrow road climbs further through the Black Mountains' open grouse moors.

---

1   https://www.walesonline.co.uk/news/wales-news/dead-birds-prey-found-estate-11853785
2   https://www.theguardian.com/uk-news/2021/aug/01/prince-harry-should-settle-bird-shooting-mystery-in-memoirs-say-campaigners

The road soon summits, and there's time for a short walk in these sunlit wilderness uplands. Red kites hang in updraughts and look for carrion. (*Photo 1*) Wild Welsh ponies with this year's foals roam free, reluctant to leave their moorland tracks. The odd swallow, still catching flies, heads off on an incredible journey to South Africa. It is peaceful, serene, up here, until a curlew's spine-chilling, bugle call echoes off the hills. Nature at its finest and most free.

The twisting road slowly descends the southern edge of the Black Mountains. Wild, open grasslands give way to a small tree-lined gulley and brook. Streams such as this one off the Beacons are home to a variety of wildlife, including elusive small brown trout, dippers and grey wagtails.

The clock tells me I am in no rush, and the anticipation of a good coffee before Cowbridge plays its timely reminder. Here, in the middle of nowhere, I would happily settle for an Instant. Further down the road, a few buildings, then a road sign, Brynamman. An old coal-mining town, one of the many that Thatcher took her axe to in the 1980s.

Grey pebble-dashed terraced houses line the road, with black, sentry-like numbered wheelie bins at front doors. Two young mums push their kids to a small park with a single swing. The same stream off the mountain runs alongside the play area. A squeal of delight from a youngster breaks the silence as she feeds a tame mallard with dry, leftover bread.

A stray dog wanders over the potholed road. Brynamman is a place the world has ignored. No coffee here ... Then blow me, a Costa sign, all of 2 feet high on a building with a shrub-infested old veranda.

'Blimey,' I muse. 'Luck's in! Even a Costa will do.'

Park the car and lock all valuables in the boot. A cock blackbird sings high in a beech tree and watches me cross the road.

The virulent song of a wren welcomes me up the path to what I am expecting to be a café of sorts, but it's an old pub. In its dimly lit interior, I see two middle-aged, overweight guys at the bar giving it all, no doubt agreeing to all the reports coming from a large TV screen tuned to Sky News. There's a pool table in one of the three rooms and seven (yes *seven*) mud-splattered parked motorbikes scattered through the large lounges as if abandoned mid-scramble. They look roadworthy but in need of a good clean. Not too dissimilar to the pub. There's a Triumph near the telly, a couple of BMWs and, in pride of place as if it guards the pool table, a Harley.

The bar is tended by a petite but confident young lady of around 20. She puts down her yellow polystyrene take-away tray of chips and curry sauce and asks in her loud, brassy, singy-song voice, 'You orrright, lovely?'

'Yes, thanks. I saw the sign for coffee.'

She can see the bemused look on my face. There is no barista-style coffee machine in sight.

'Here you are, lovely,' she says, passing me a cup, a cartridge of coffee and a carton of milk. She points to a machine no bigger than 9 inches tall sitting in a dark corner of the room: 'Just help yourself, dear.'

I must look as blank as I often do. She puts her tray down again, comes out from behind the bar, and kindly makes my coffee.

Well, it isn't the best, but it would be rude to leave. Sitting there I take in the scene, trying, and failing miserably, to blend in.

Time to look more closely at the bikes with all their paraphernalia, when suddenly two young boys burst into the gloom, brightening the room with the daylight from the open door. The elder of the two – he looks about 12, slightly overweight – carries an old, worn car tyre. Talking loudly above the television, he stands there confidently: 'All right, everyone I'm only asking £1 for this tyre. Come on, be quick! I'm not going to stand here all day.'

No takers, and off the two go, a fine example of the splendid audacity of youth.

The coffee supped, it's time to leave. At the bar, Stacey noshes away and answers her mobile phone. No privacy is wanted or expected, but her megaphone voice and comments are surreal. Every reply of hers ends in 'never'. Is that an opinion or a question?

Geographically it's a small journey over the Beacons, but it's a huge journey for many; from royal courtiers with their protected grouse moors and ancestral fishing rights to humble, coalmining valley folk trying to eke out a decent life where jobs are somewhere between scarce and non-existent.

Next door to the pub is a derelict, fire-damaged house with no roof. Charred timbers and blackened masonry. Saplings have taken root, spreading up through the first floor's seared joists. Nettles grow tall in concrete cracks, and house sparrows chirp their friendly song amongst the fired bricks. Left alone, nature will take over completely. It will take time, but she has time. Wilderness it is not yet, but wild it is.

The walk back to the car; two buzzards circle each other on a thermal, a kestrel hovers high, and a couple of crows squabble in the wet ruts of an old drovers' track leading back up the Black Mountains. Nature is all around, everywhere, especially where humans have trodden lightly.

Bruce Kendrick, summer 2017

I

THINGWALL

He cuts a middle-aged, scholarly figure. Dark-rimmed glasses with bulbous lenses, black suit, white shirt, light blue tie and shiny black shoes. He opens his brown medical bag with its single brass lock and worn handle, and takes out his stethoscope to listen yet again to my chest.

'Breathe deeply,' he says, tapping away on the two fingers he places over my chest and upper back. He repeats these soundings of my lungs and leaves the bedroom to have a word with Ma and Dad. It's not long before he returns to tell me in his deadpan way that he wants me to have further tests in hospital.

It's a hot and sticky May afternoon, 1957, and the street on the estate is silent. Children are at school. Husbands are at work. I am wrapped in a light brown patterned woollen blanket, a weak ten-year-old lad carried unseen, by his Dad out to the waiting Bedford ambulance with its pale green and white livery. The driver makes me comfortable on the trolley bed. Dad sits nearby. We move off slowly. Upstairs terrace windows pass by, their lace curtains offering a uniform privacy, before sleep creeps on.

I come round as the ambulance brakes and finally stops at Birkenhead Children's Hospital. Staff are primed, waiting at the front door. I am wheeled immediately into radiography for lung X-rays and then taken to a made-up bed on the second floor in a quiet corner of a boys' ward.

Faded, pale green curtains are drawn around the bed, and medical staff congregate, led by Dr Banerjee. The X-ray negatives are held up against the light. Fingers point. After 20 minutes of further examination

1

and discussions, the doctor's entourage, in their assorted white coats, slowly shuffle away to continue their deliberations.[3] The curtains are drawn back, and nurses make me comfortable. Confused and tired, I don't know what to make of it all.

I ask, 'Which ward am I in?'

'You're in the medical ward, which means you'll be treated with medicine, not surgery.'

Is that good? Should I be pleased? The idea of surgery sounds unpleasant, dangerous. Life-threatening?

Dr Banerjee visits three times a day, checking my vital signs. Medication is prescribed and further tests are carried out, including a procedure to involve a very large needle being stuck into my body between two ribs to take a lung sample. The nurses have precise instructions to enter my chest between the third and fourth ribs.

They check several times to make sure. 'This might be painful.'

It is.

Three weeks pass. I should be missing home, but there's a part of me which readily accepts it all; I'm here and that's it. There's little I can do but wait. At no time do I suspect I'm extremely ill. Usually, young kids can't get their minds round the idea of mortality, and of course nursing staff and parents offer positive vibes. Life stretches ahead for ever.

It is a new world, though, an isolated world where days have unique routines and shapes, where hospital time has different, distinct patterns.

Dad has the highest praise for Dr Banerjee, telling me he is the very best.

'You have pleural effusion,' says Dad. 'You need a specialised hospital which can take very good care of you. It might take a while before you're completely better.'

A move to Thingwall Sanatorium is organised. The word 'sanatorium' sounds permanent, cheerless. A place for the long-term poorly. Where's Thingwall?

This time the view from the ambulance is of orderly semi-detached houses, each with their neat gardens and garages, net curtains as in our street but with posh white fascia boards and gable ends. Tidy. This is

---

3   Apparently my first 24 hours in hospital were critical. Little did I realise at the time, but when I was admitted with only a third of a lung working it was touch and go for me.

Woodchurch Road in Birkenhead's southern suburbs. At Arrowe Park's crossroads, the ambulance heads south into the Wirral countryside. A metal pole announces a plethora of village names which all end in 'by': Frankby, Irby, Greasby, Pensby and West Kirby.

Past the cemetery at Landican. Small, irregular green fields. Dairy pastures, hedge-trimmed in hawthorn, still draped in the remnants of faded white blossom. Crows cavort above the crown of a mature oak as a shaft of bright light falls on a herd of Friesians. A fancy, a chimera of a daydream, plays games with this bucolic scene. A hidden voice says, 'Stay with us. You'll be safe here. Come home. We'll get you better.'

The ambulance turns off the main road into a peaceful lane in need of repair. Two thatched cottages sit back from the unmade road. In places, the ambulance carefully follows the indentations of rutted scars where the traffic, probably the metal rims of old farm carts, has cut into red sandstone.

Looking back up the lane from the ambulance I can see a grass mound rise above the tall hawthorn hedge. 'This is Thingwall, then?' I ask myself. To my child's eye, the uniform, shallow conical shape of the mound looks man-made and suggests a previous epoch, a time of before, a time of fables.

A sudden swerve by the ambulance avoids a kit rabbit darting across our path. A pair of weather-worn sandstone pillars straddle the lane, where iron gates, painted black, hang permanently open on their hinges. Such is the stranglehold of nettles and brambles.

The ambulance crosses the threshold, descends a twisting path before it stops in a wide clearing. A large gravel parking area surrounds a collection of rectangular single-storey buildings. Horizontal timber cladding, now silvery-grey, runs the length of the buildings, like a well-worn coat which has seen better days. Wooden window frames and doors are painted a dull dark brown. All set in orangey-red brick framework.

The buildings are large lived-in huts, more intimate than the children's hospital, set against tall, friendly trees. This is rustic Cheshire. This is isolated rustic Cheshire.

No drama of an emergency arrival, no rushing for x-rays, just the friendly faces of a small welcoming committee, a nurse and a sister.

Two wards, one for boys, one for girls, of ten beds each, set at right angles to each other off a central administration area. My new bed awaits in a corner cut off from the rest of the ward. A reminder for me to always stay in bed, apart from occasional trips to the toilet and bathroom. A few boys are sitting up, but most are asleep.

There is a gentle, soft, restful peace here. You can touch it. This place knows what it must do. Unobserved, it gets on with it. No fuss.

The nursing staff wear colour-coded uniforms, black stockings and soft, flat shoes which grip and squeak on spotlessly clean, polished parquet floors. Orderlies, in light brown and starched-stiff linen caps, clean and feed us. Ward nurses wear green, and the tall, slim, blonde ward sister looks magnificent, almost regal, in navy blue, her white tiara an intricately folded linen voile, held in place with a couple of hairclips.

The beds are enormous. Gunmetal, tubular frames and rounded corners, each bedstead moored to an allocated berth, anchored to the floor by foot-operated pedals on all four castors. Bed linen of starched white sheets, large fluffy pillows and faded yellowy-brown woollen blankets. Two clipboards hanging at the end of every bed showing graphs of temperature readings, pulse rates, bowel movements (numbers 1 and 2) and other notes taken four times a day by nurses in green. A yellowing, wooden bedside cabinet, the height of the bed's headrest, to carry a few personal possessions: a couple of books, a well-thumbed comic, a box of tissues and always a tumbler of water. A few Get Well cards, brought from the previous hospital, standing dutifully upright.

A small, unflappable isolation hospital existing in its own private bubble. The outside world is unaware we are here. Our private, daily routines revolve around the primary needs of prescribed pharmacology and the quotidian evidence of pulse counts and thermometer readings.

The day starts at six in the morning when floor to ceiling curtains are drawn, allowing soft primal light to flood in through large, glass-paned, wooden veranda doors. The morning's routine slowly kicks in. Recent admissions are not allowed to the toilets, so bed pans are circulated, and privacy restored when screens are trundled out. Bed washes follow, then a breakfast of cereals and fruit in coloured plastic bowls, toast with a tumbler of juice.

Time for medication before the rest of the day, the quiet.

Many of the 20 or so very ill kids have afternoon sessions to cough up phlegm into a waiting empty bowl on the floor near their bed. They lie face down whilst nurses aggressively slap their backs.[4] I feel for them. A few cry. It does not strike me that I'm weak like them, but then what do I know? I'm told I will get better. Isn't everyone going to get better? The children in the ward stay in their beds and do not mix.

Days are placid and peaceful. Days repeat. No background radio babble, just the soft voices of the nursing staff. The occasional soft, catlike, purring sounds of pigeons, from the wood opposite creep into our days, breaking the routine silence.

Tall concertina-hinged doors, long, narrow windows, high up near the ceiling, run the length of the ward. A long pole with a small metal hook stands in the corner, ready to open these skylights to provide fresh air. If the weather is warm and dry, our bedsteads, like rows of metal skiffs, are untethered from the parquet floor. With the help of a gentle push, the beds float out onto the veranda's flat, concrete terrace. The welcoming fragrance of laundered white bed sheets and the feel of their smooth, freshly starched surface do their best to provide comfort against nature's elements. As I write these lines 60 years later, I can conjure up the feel of those linen sheets, and they carry a soft lilac smell, with hints of vanilla. They take me back; Gran had a purple lilac bush in her garden whose flowers were brushed by the gate as you opened it. I was born in her house.

Waking up to early morning rain means a day indoors. Once the daily medical procedures are done, there is little to do other than read, eat and sleep. It is after all a regime of medication and strict bed rest. Every day a slow, sure day.

One night my sleep is poor. Soon after dusk, owls hoot and screech in the near wood. The wind is up, the windows open. One individual shriek sends shivers. When the curtains are drawn in the morning, a close scattering, no more than 2 feet across, of small, pink and white downy feathers form a neat circle on the adjacent green lawn, still damp from dew. Several feathers have red stains.

Visiting time, normally 2 p.m., is controlled with military precision. Parents can be seen in the waiting area behind the ward's double doors.

---

4   The resulting sputum is sent off to identify any tell-tale bacteria.

At 2 p.m. precisely the doors open; we all look up expectantly, to see if we have visitors. Each boy is allowed two adults but no siblings. I'm a lucky lad as I get at least one visitor every day. Often it is Ma, as Dad can't get from his work to the hospital unless it's a weekend. When he does make it, he often chats to youngsters who do not have company,

Every visit brings a gift from Ma, even if it's just a tube of Polo mints, an apple or orange. A red-letter day means a comic. A clear favourite is Dan Dare's weekly adventures in the *Eagle*. Books are a treat, too. I take a shine to Arthur Ransome's adventure stories in the Swallows and Amazons series. I have three in my bedside locker. Dad brings *The Three Musketeers* by Alexander Dumas, a beautiful edition in an embossed blue leather-effect covers. He says it's a boy's adventure book. After a few pages it stays unread.

A handbell is rung, the signal there are five minutes left to the hour-long visit. A tinge of homesickness descends as parents stroll out through those double doors, taking their world with them. The ward takes on its own brief, tangible melancholia. Nurses quickly circulate, offering comfort to the few that are upset, crying silently under the covers.

Little moves outside. A few birds flit from branch to branch and occasionally an inquisitive rabbit sniffs the breeze. The swaying, waving motion of the tallest trees, standing proud out there, mesmerise and invite.

Breakfast has just been served when the gardener, a weekly visitor in his dark overalls and a black French beret, worn to one side of his head, arrives on the lawn nearest the wood, clasping a long-handled scythe. He scrupulously sharpens the elongated, curved cutting edge with what looks like a smooth stone. He checks its sharpness by drawing his thumb across the blade. Satisfied, he twists his back, and with just a handful of deep metronomic sweeps, like a relentless pendulum, he silently works the overgrown near edge of the wood. A few boys cough. He rakes the loose, dead stems into a pile and walks out of vision.

A few minutes later, the engine noise of his mower presages his return. He walks the big grass cutter to and fro across the green lawn. The sweet, phosgene smell of newly mown grass seeps through the ward's open windows. A blackbird with a bright yellow beak watches from a favourite limb, no doubt hoping for a juicy worm.

A rabbit ventures onto the newly cut sward. She holds her nose up to whiff the air before she nibbles on young shoots and clover. Her head is upright, her nose twitches those delicate whiskers. The doe is disturbed. Her round brown eyes spot danger and she's off into the safety of the wood.

During visiting, I mention to Dad I have seen a few birds when I've been out on the veranda.

'Really? What were they?'

'No idea, but they were small and blue and yellow. Another one with a red front came down to feed on worms on the ground, and there was a blackbird watching a rabbit feed on the grass, just there.' I point to the spot.

'The bird with a red chest could be a robin,' he says.

It's the end of August, my 11th birthday. My present is a small, carefully wrapped parcel. It's *The Observer's Book of Birds*, a pocket-size book with illustrations, mainly monochrome, and descriptions of 236 species of birds. We look at it together and try to find the little blue and yellow bird.

Birds are grouped by family, with strange names: *corvidae* for crows, *fringillidae* for finches and buntings, *alaudidae* for larks and so on.

'That's Latin,' Dad says.

One bird per page, each with a brief description of identifying features and measurements. A few words on haunts, nest, eggs, food and calls. A book to dip into. The little blue and yellow bird in the illustration on page 66 of my new book is a blue tit in typical upside-down pose, hanging from a twig of what can only be described as a drab shrub. The blue tit to be seen from my bed when out on the terrace looks brighter: pale, azure blues and lemon yellows, feeding from a saucer of scraps on a home-made bird table. (*Photo 2*)

A few days later, clutching my *Observer's Book* I try to identify a few different avian visitors to the veranda's fringe. Great tits with their large black stripe down their yellow bellies like a circus clown's outfit. From a bush comes a loud, noisy warble, and soon a posturing wren makes a brief appearance. Surely that little bird is too small to make such loud noise? A singing blackbird sits brazenly at the top of a bush.

The ward sister in her smart royal blue takes an interest. She has a soft, beautiful smile and always asks about my birds. I learn more to impress.

Her occasional visits are always accompanied by the fragrance of her delicate perfume.

She sits neatly on the edge of the bed with her legs crossed. 'Hello, Bruce. How are you today? What have you seen this morning?'

'Just the usual, Sister. But I did see a wren yesterday.'

'They are so little, but they make a lot of noise,' she says, adjusting her navy blue skirt so that it lies neatly, showing her knees. My young eyes linger on the shiny, fine denier mesh of her black stockings.

It's late August; the raucous cackle of a couple of quarrelling magpies breaks through the tight foliage of the wood.

A hen blackbird feels obliged to descend to the ground to sound her sharp alarm call, a threatening and agitated 'pink, pink'. Her tail almost upright, she flicks her wings as if in annoyance and stands boldly; her wing tips touch the grass. Whatever danger she has spotted passes. She resumes her search for worms in the soft turf.

Autumn arrives slowly. Winds pick up, trees shake and bend. Leaves fade to burnt yellows and ochres as harvest colours descend upon the woods. A few desiccated leaves drift past the windows, tossed by the breeze before settling on the turf. Days grow shorter and cooler. The lights still come on at six in the morning but it's dark outside. The inexorable routine continues, letting medication work its slow, sure momentum.

One November afternoon, the gorgeous blonde sister comes and sits, cross-legged on my bed. My eyes turn again to the sheer denier of her black stockings. Are these different, a finer denier perhaps? They seem more transparent.

She spots me looking at her legs and I blush. She smiles a knowing smile and says, 'Now Bruce, the doctor's next routine visit will be tomorrow. You should ask him when he thinks you'll be going home.'

I take on board her suggestion, but it carries no significance. I am not counting days, and the thought of not going home does not trouble me. Tomorrow arrives without excitement; yet another day like all the ones that have gone before. The ward is even more spotless than usual. It's mid-morning when the white-coated doctor begins his round. I'm fourth or fifth in his routine when he arrives at my bed.

I sit up and the sister says, 'Now, Bruce, don't you have a question for the doctor?'

I have completely forgotten. I choose my words carefully, as I have one of those stammers where it's difficult to say a few specific words. I normally manage by finding an alternative well in advance. The word 'when' is one of them, so I try it out in my mind first.

'Oh yes. [When] do you think I may go home, please?'

'Well, let me see. Yes, it all looks fine. Monday,' he replies.

Overjoyed, I look up to the beautiful sister. She gives me the most wonderful disarming, radiant smile. She sits down beside me and holds my hand. I disappear under the sheets and weep a few unseen tears.

So my safe sojourn at the NHS's wonderful hospitality and life-saving service comes to a very positive end. I will miss the sister. Six months in an isolation bed is a long time for an 11-year-old.

A visit every single day for six months. Not one day missed. Thingwall is 6 miles away from our council house in Leasowe. I know now it was Ma who came every day. What I find extraordinary is she did not rely on public transport. My parents did not drive and there was no spare cash. Help was at hand, however, within the family; she had borrowed a bike from her brother-in-law, Albert, who we all knew as Uncle Ken. On many occasions she rode the 12-mile return journey. Surely there must have been times she used the buses when the weather was bad. Dad, an emergency-trained post-war teacher, came to visit at weekends and in school holidays.

The sanatorium at Thingwall is no longer there. It was knocked down to build a private hospital. The same can't be said of the disease it treated all those years ago. There's a popular misconception that tuberculosis has been eradicated. Not so. Recent figures from NHS England show a peak in reported cases of 8,280 in 2011 which then steadily reduced to 4,672 in 2018. The report also said that 40 per cent of cases were in London, but these figures make few headlines. The numbers are at best disconcerting, at worst frightening.

Many of those who carry the bacterium today live in our society's margins. Destitute, homeless folk, whose immune systems are shot. Those with addiction problems are especially at risk. Many of those in shelters and halfway houses unknowingly carry the infection. To tackle this problem there is an NHS mobile X-ray unit, touring those London postcodes thought to be high risk areas, using the innocuous title 'Find and Treat'. TB now hides in plain sight. Social attitudes have changed little since 1957.

I caught the bacterium from my mild-mannered maternal grandad who stayed with us for a month when he was temporarily homeless. His bed was put next to mine. He'd been a rigger in the merchant navy, working in the Arctic. His health suffered. My Ma was born in 1924 and is called Olga Dorothy. A Russian lady friend perhaps?

Dad chose his words carefully when he told me, in hospital, that I had pleural effusion.

I have since read the medical literature concerning pleural effusion. The pleura are thin membranes that cover the surface of our lungs and the inside of our chest wall, and pleural effusion is too much fluid collecting in the pleura. The fluid shows up white on a chest x-ray. The condition is often described as 'water on the lungs', and it can be caused by several illnesses, including pneumonia and tuberculosis. So technically Dad was correct, but economical with the truth.

My guess is he killed two birds with one brick, as they say in our parts. Tuberculosis was seen then as a disease of the poor, and by using this euphemism Dad both avoided his own embarrassment and gave me hope. I wonder if this was a strategy agreed with Dr Banerjee and the hospital medical staff?

In fact, this elephant stayed in the room for many years. It was not discussed at home and sometimes carefully avoided. I knew I had been very poorly, but I used the term 'pleural effusion' if anyone asked. I had my suspicions in my early teens, when I was excused the mass BCG vaccine, but it was my GP, Tony, who finally confirmed tuberculosis. I was in my forties. He looked at my voluminous medical notes and quoted a section that described how a guinea pig had been injected with fluid extracted from my lungs via that painful procedure. It died of TB.

Tuberculosis has been around for 17,000 years but we have moved on from using harrowing and dreaded terms such as consumption, scrofula and Pott's disease. Even as late as the 1950s, the 'poor plague', as it was also called, could still reach out and take a life within three weeks of a first strike. Little did I know as a lad the role tuberculosis had played in my forebears: TB had orphaned my paternal grandfather, George, when he was 14, and had already killed both his grandparents, my great-great-grandparents. The men were wheelwright labourers from the West Midlands. They all died in the workhouse. TB finally caught up with my maternal grandad, who gave me the infection. He died in his sixties.

Clean, fresh air is important to those with lung complaints. Putting a sanatorium in a wooded location is not an accident. During daylight hours the complex biological processes behind photosynthesis absorb carbon dioxide from our atmosphere and release oxygen. Plants and trees don't breathe as such – they don't have lungs – but wooded areas create oxygen-rich surroundings ideal for patients with respiratory problems. Opening the large veranda doors in the middle of those woods ensures maximum exposure to whatever extra oxygen there might be.

It was standard medical practice in the mid-fifties to confine the patient to bed for six months (in my case, to the day) whilst the medicines and other procedures did their slow, deliberate work.

Did the long stint in an isolation hospital at the age of ten affect how I began to see the world around me? What other invisible, formative threads are to be traced back to those days of fresh air, isolation and slow recovery?

On the physical front, all sports are out of the question until I am 14. I reluctantly join a small and ignominious group of boys who have notes from mothers asking they be excluded from games and gym. Already a bit of an outsider, perhaps?

Early teenage years coincide with the beginnings of the sixties counterculture. The young question the establishment, the status quo. New ideas spread in the social norms of music, clothes, and of course Mary Jane shows up at a few parties. More importantly, attitudes to the establishment change. Authority is challenged, and that appeals. Youngsters re-evaluate their lot. Mass student sit-down protests, Flower-power, the beginnings of feminism and anti-nuclear demonstrations reflect this social flux. A few of us are caught up in these highly politicised margins.

I'm not the only one to see injustices.

Our 9-inch Bush television carries grainy black and white BBC news coverage of Ban the Bomb marches. The image slips and disappears off the bottom of the screen, only to reappear at the top before slipping again. This infuriating rolling repeats until you twiddle the vertical hold knob, located somewhere at the back of the set. It only takes a minor, but frequent, adjustment until the set warms up and settles down.

Over Easter the annual march from the home of the Atomic Weapons Establishment, Aldermaston, to Trafalgar Square gets plenty of airtime. The same little television also shows horrific mushroom-cloud pictures of atmospheric nuclear tests in the Pacific.

The young gather to protest as never before. The Campaign for Nuclear Disarmament, CND, has charismatic leaders such as the leading British analytical philosopher Professor Bertrand Russell and a radical Roman Catholic priest by the name of Monsignor Bruce Kent – an unholy alliance, attracting many public figures and eminent scholars. I'm active in my local CND branch, go on demos, marches and sit-downs, and am the only kid in a school of 350 to wear my lapel badge to school with pride, confirming, perhaps, the outsider tag. Is it around this time that my stammer decides to go and bother someone else?

For 13 days in October 1962, at the height of the Cuban missile crisis, the superpowers of America and Russia are involved in a stand-off which could so easily lead to nuclear war. It's a Wednesday afternoon and our rugby match is over. I ask Mr Armitage, a teacher, if there is any news. Has Nikita Khrushchev backed down? He looks down at me carefully over his specs and says, 'You are not to worry,' but his eyes tell another tale. He's clearly concerned that a young 16-year-old has such dark, heavy thoughts.

Were these anxieties of Armageddon related to the hospital stay and being so very ill? I have always suspected a connection, however flimsy. A fine thread, translucent perhaps, which recognises our individual mortality.

I'm 22 when I take my first proper job, working in a factory in Ernesettle in Plymouth as an electronic engineer for the Rank Organisation, making Bush Murphy colour televisions.

All my student jobs used to pay me cash in a weekly wage packet, and I have a Post Office account to bank any spare pennies. But this new job pays a monthly salary direct into a bank account. The personnel department strongly suggests I get myself a bank account. So off I trot to the National Westminster Bank in Plymouth and ask for an account. Surely it would be quite straightforward. Surely it would like to have my money, just like the Post Office. An interview with a manager soon puts me right: in order to open an account, I need two character references as well as proof of my identity and address.

'Character references. What are they?' I ask.

'Well, two individuals who will vouch for your good character,' the manager replies, 'but not just anyone like a neighbour or a relative. We need independent, upright citizens like doctors, vicars, magistrates, police officers or judges.'

'Crikey,' I say to myself, 'I know a few coppers who knocked me about on sit-downs. I know a magistrate, but I was looking at him across the dock as a 16-year-old, and I certainly don't know a judge or a vicar.'

'I've only just arrived in Plymouth, and still have to find a doctor,' I tell the manager. 'I might find that difficult.'

'No problem,' he says. 'It'll just take longer.'

Two weeks later he phones me at work. 'Good news; your account is set up. All we need is for you to come to the bank whenever it's convenient, so we can complete the formalities.'

That afternoon I take the bus from Ernesettle into the middle of Plymouth, a pleasant half-hour ride. The young manager guides me into a small, empty meeting room with a desk and two chairs. He's carrying all the relevant paperwork as well as a separate buff foolscap envelope tucked under his left arm. He goes through the account details. I give him a specimen signature and take hold of the cheque book.

I'm about to leave when he says, 'You may want to take a look at what's in this.' He rests the envelope on the empty desk. 'As you weren't able to offer any character references, we had to do a little digging ourselves. I have another meeting, but please just leave this envelope on the desk and I'll collect it later.'

Intrigued, of course, I open the buff envelope – and there on a single piece of foolscap are details of my involvement with CND, dates of sit-downs outside St George's Hall in Liverpool, and my brief time in other left-wing activities, all considered a threat to national security. Like many others of my generation, I have an MI5 file. The establishment views me as a possible threat to national security and banks have access to its files.

Of course, it's all changed now.

2

SAND PLOUGHMAN

The consultant at the sanatorium suggests that Switzerland's fine air and spa waters will aid further recovery. Once we master the spelling, we eventually find Switzerland on a map. Our home library consists of a dictionary, the atlas in question and a few of Dad's Isaac Asimov paperbacks.[5] Switzerland is miles away. Countries away. It might as well be on another planet.

The consultant has, knowingly, suggested that if Switzerland is not possible, then a more viable plan is to go to the coast where air is fresh and clean. He explains that seashores are home to ozone with its extra atom of oxygen, O_3, as opposed to the normal two atoms, O_2.[6] Fortunately at Leasowe, where we live, the shore is just a 15-minute walk from our house.

We live near the shore but we cannot see the sea. In the way is a stretch of sandhills. The name Leasowe is an Anglo-Saxon word meaning 'meadow pastures'. We live at or just below sea-level. An area prone to flooding.[7]

---

5 Isaac Azimov (1920–1992) was a Russian-born American biochemist who was a prolific writer of both fiction and non-fiction. He is often quoted, but this one I like. It has touches of Plato: 'Anti-intellectualism has been a constant thread winding its way through our political and cultural life, nurtured by the false notion that democracy means that "my ignorance is just as good as your knowledge"'.

6 Modern science suggests there is no appreciable difference in the amount of ozone on our shorelines as against elsewhere.

7 Leasowe is at or below sea level, and is protected by the coastal embankment. Houses built in the early 20th century were often flooded and unsanitary, but after 1926 new roads and drainage were built by the borough council.

Close the blue front door, turn left on Cook Road, right into Raleigh, left again into Gardenside, past the new, uninspiring, red brick Catholic church and then cross the main road. So far so good.

Feelings of anxiety first intrude when I see the dark entrance to the unmarked narrow footpath leading to the sand dunes. Beyond the dunes is the shore. A neighbour has told me of a local legend; this lane is haunted by the ghost of a Leasowe wrecker carrying a lantern.

The opening in the tall hawthorn hedge is cramped. Ten yards from the dark entrance the track morphs into a tunnel made by untrimmed hedges on either side where bramble, privet and hawthorn meet at head height and fight for light.

Anxious and alone for the first time on this damp footpath. I'm frightened a little and begin to sweat. I can see daylight ahead and quicken my steps. It helps that the cindered path is ruler-straight. After 100 yards the dark, tight passage widens and forms one of many lanes which criss-cross these pastures. All paths lead to a handful of market gardens.

A wooden gate opens onto an open, lush green pasture, strewn with yellow ragwort, cowslip and fresh crumpled molehills. It's wet underfoot, waterlogged in places, and for the first time I inhale the gentle sea breeze wafting over the dunes, carrying hints of old geraniums, iodine and rotten seaweed.

A friendly at-home robin trills from a bordering blackthorn. A faint trodden trace of an animal track meanders across the damp pasture for 100 yards before passing through a fence of sorts, now short of a few palings, space enough for a young lad to crawl through. It then climbs to the sandhills before vanishing in the dunes. After another 100 yards dunes give way to a crumbling, sea-torn concrete embankment which has seen better days. This is Leasowe shore. Turn right and the embankment will take you on solid ground all the way to Wallasey Village and New Brighton. Turn left and the embankment is no more, washed away in recent gales; it is now a shallow bay 100 yards across, littered with concrete debris, sandstone rubble, tidal pools and rippled sands.

It is nine months since I looked out from the cosy security of a hospital bed on the veranda's edge, close to the cropped green lawn and leafy wood. It was like sitting alone in the private box of a small theatre where the set is a painted, pastoral scene from an old master. Safe, but artificial.

The world is different now. Leasowe shore is for real. Dark lanes, wide-open soggy pastures, muddy tidal waters, brittle sand dunes, high seas, collapsed embankments, far horizons. Gone is the contentment of the sanatorium's safe, cocooned solitude.

Successive visits slowly calm the natural fears of the unknown. It takes time for me to adjust and feel comfortable again. Reassuringly, home is just 15 minutes away – but there is that stretch of the dark footpath to retread.

Dad's birthday present, in hospital, of the little bird book was his way of helping me pass the time but it turns out to be a catalyst; a not-so secret door into another dimension. *The Observer's Book of Birds* becomes a long list to be ticked. It's undeniable that many folk like to collect, and I too carry the bug. The youngster's spark of a stickler's curiosity slowly fashions and forms into a lifelong appreciation of nature's wonder. Why do I and others get so much pleasure out of simply observing animals and birds?

It helps when one person, over time, becomes four. I meet three budding birdwatchers at school. I'm not sure how we got together. Memory is blank on that one. Maybe it was the school's natural history society? There was no one moment when the friendship started. A motley gang of four lads from different parts of Wallasey drift together through a passion for birding: Mac, Bob, Roy and me.

Mac is tallest. A bit of an all-round athlete. A good cross-country runner and a fly-half in the rugby team. Whenever everyone else is rushing for their bus home, you will find Mac practising kicking the oval ball between the two white posts on the school's playing fields. Blond hair and blue eyes. He's got the lot. Girls think so as well. Certainly not the stereotypical image of an introverted teenage birder.

Bob is the bright spark amongst us. Top of his class in the school's A stream. Modest, though. One of those who infuriatingly glides through exams effortlessly while the rest of us revise, revise, revise. When Bob applies to Oxford as a 17-year-old, a teacher spots that he does not have the obligatory Latin O level. No problem. He passes the Latin exam with top marks after one year of extra studies. He's not a swot; he's just naturally very clever. He can draw, too. Bastard.

Roy's initial interest in nature was botany and pond life, but birds are fine too. Like Mac he plays rugby, but unlike Mac he refuses to train. Mac and Roy share biology classes and a social life. Roy's other passion is sailing.

We scribble down in our little black notebooks the names of the birds we see and any accompanying notes of interest. The pedant's list.

Black notebooks grow into a collection kept in an old shoebox under the bed. Notebooks provide a home for lists but also offer a place to contemplate. The word 'why' often starts a reflection. Why did all the gulls today move west along the shore? Why were the oystercatchers not in their usual haunt? The answers are rarely to be found in the two reference books I have in my bedroom.[8] Most school homework can wait, but not maths as I'm scared stiff of the maths teacher.

A deeper understanding of our patch builds slowly. There's an inverse relationship between the confidence that comes from familiarity and early anxieties about new and vast open spaces.

We learn to approach key locations with care; last time we flushed a few snipe from this patch of swampy damp grass. Check distant fence lines for anything out of the ordinary. Where to find what? Which behaviour patterns are likely to repeat?

A close affinity with this private new world builds intimacy, attachment and a belonging. Even the dark rakes become friends.[9]

A sheltered grassy bank overlooks a pool where moorhen stagger and jerk across the surface, where damselflies, like jewelled gossamer fairies, dart. A windbreak of tall sedge offers protection for hidden wrens to blast out their noisy, limited repertoire. A narrow dyke crosses a meadow where kingfisher flash, leaving a strident turquoise trace. Meadow brown butterflies flutter and settle to feed on flower heads in the rays of midday. A dense reed bed hosts a pair of squealing water rail, and several sedge warblers call from bulrushes. A field corner where a few circumspect skylarks skulk in stubble. In late spring, horse paddocks attract migrating yellow wagtails, their canary colours matching the meadow's gilded buttercups.

---

8   *The Observer's Book of Birds*, and *The Popular Handbook of British Birds* by P.A.D. Hollom.
9   The local name 'rake' is Norse for a lane. One of Wallasey's roads is called Rake Lane, which literally means 'lane lane'.

Corn buntings sing their song of jangling keys. A willow's canopy is cover for a calling chiffchaff. Silky sounds of early summer.

The Wirral being a peninsula, the sea is never far away. Our patch is its 7-mile north shore. When everyone else inland has the calm, windless days of summer, here is always a breeze, either onshore or offshore depending on the time of day.

Cold seas of spring and early summer have the effect of cooling the peninsula by a couple of degrees. As summer progresses seas warm; temperatures peak in late August, and their relative warmth lasts into the early winter months, taking the edge off the early winter cold – more of a chill, then. But January and February can be severely cold; by then the seas have cooled again.

We learn how the patch moves on and changes with each incoming season. Its moods. We begin, not that we know it yet, to understand a little of nature's deep rhythms and chords.[10]

Some days lodge themselves in our mind to be remembered as if they were just yesterday.

SPRING

A bright day in late April: the narrow footpath is dressed in white blossom. Cross the drier meadow. Saunter through the sandhills to the shore where high tide laps gently against the slope of the scarred concrete embankment. Placid, washing waves which invite a safe discovery of a pelagic vastness. Waves gently wash, surge and swell. Devoid of any threatening intent, they simply caress and solicit, slosh and ripple. They whisper to anyone who can hear, 'We are soft, at the command of the sea, but we fuse with unknown, distant shell-strewn shores.'

A lazy herring gull drifts gracefully by, lifted and bathed by the gentle breeze. The bird looks at me quizzically, pointing its yellow beak my way. A true master of its own world. Bobbing by is an ocean-worn, battered blue plastic drum, no bigger than our coal scuttle.

It is calm, but towering cumulonimbus, moisture cargo clouds, bubble and froth in the far west. A thunderhead perhaps?

The tide and crosscurrents begin their gentle dance, afternoon throes

---

10 I understand now what Shakespeare meant when he wrote 'the earth has music for those who listen'.

of a slow maritime waltz. Lazy ripples scar the surface. Whirls froth where undertow clings to the embankment. Tidal currents play eddies in deeper water.

A black-headed gull, with the beginnings of its summer plumage of a chocolate brown – not black – head, lands in the gentle turmoil to grab a small fish, glistening silver in the slow ferment. A second black-headed gull, still in winter plumage, makes a din, harrying the first gull. The leading gull swerves, swivels and climbs 20 feet, but the second gull won't back off, mirroring every twist and turn. The white leading edge to their wings contrasts sharply with the dark cloud backdrop. (*Photo 3*) The commotion attracts a third gull. It's too much for the leading gull. The shiny minnow slips from its beak and one of the two chasing gulls dives down to the surface, opens its scarlet gape, scoops the prize and flies off.

Turbulence arrives in the form of marine eruptions as moist winds freshen. There is a new brightness to the sea. Surface water glistens in the soft light, changing colours as it swells and sways. Wafts of salinity, iodine and rotten seaweed add their sensual overture.

Storm clouds are soon upon us. The expanse of the Irish Sea, from Liverpool through to North Wales, begins to tilt and twist. Strong winds shear wave crests, creating tumbling white horses. A few yards from where we stand, green algae covers the slope, waving gently in the high tide. Spindrift carries inland and settles as soft froth on clumps of spiky marram grass.

Small waders use the swell's updrafts, flying directly to where their busy wings take them. Gulls, masters of the headwind, have time to linger and pass the time of day.

Fat raindrops plop and splatter on the sea's surface. The prelude. Dark clouds, rich in moisture, are almost overhead now. Winds freshen. The downpour is upon us. Binoculars are hidden under flimsy waterproofs which cannot take much more of this battering. Time to retreat, but there's no shelter. A long, wet trudge home. Socks squelch in our leather boots.

SUMMER

Early, just after six. A clear summer's morning. A pale blue sky still carries lingering pink hints of dawn. High-altitude wisps of transparent, flimsy cirrostratus drift. We creep through the dunes to the shore. A slow climb. Sliding in fluid, failing footholds of the dry sand. Tumbledown, crumbling steep slopes.

What will we find today, what new birds might there be over the next ridge? Piping alarm calls of oystercatchers echo in the distance.

Nature's clues abound: undisturbed bird tracks in the sand, half-eaten berries, droppings, bird calls, a fanned spray of feathers from a raptor kill, probably made by a peregrine.

Temporary shelter is found in a shallow dune hollow surrounded by ramparts of spindly, razor-sharp marram grass. Above us, winding coils of thermal-riding gulls use air currents to achieve incredible heights. Soon-to-become-dots drift slowly east.

We understand little of this new world, but our scant knowledge brings a respect for nature's unconditional companionship. She's always there. We ask questions of each other. It's like peeling an onion. A layer is removed only to reveal another layer underneath. A question is answered, only for the answer to prompt another question. There's no disgrace in not knowing the answer. Nature is there to be observed. Nature is neutral. She is directed solely by her biology. We just need to understand a tad more biology.

Inland, behind the embankment, are low meadow pastures. Before the embankment's barrier was built, these leasowes (as Anglo-Saxons called them) would flood at exceptionally high tides. The soil here is a rich, dark-brown tilth. Over time pastures have been partitioned into small workable plots. Collectively these plots make up the market gardens; a croft-like business where parcels of land are passed down through family inheritance.

I work these market gardens on Saturdays and holidays for pocket money and to save up for a pair of decent binoculars.[11] Humdrum weeding. Weeding with trowels, weeding with hoes, weeding with hands, snipping out unwanted shoots of fast-growing tomatoes in long, hot greenhouses. The distinct smell of crushed green peppers carries heavily in these polythene tunnels.

---

11 After I have saved up £10 Dad suggests he pays the rest as my birthday present. The bins cost £25 in 1960, bought from the Army & Navy shop in Birkenhead. I still have them: a pair of East German Carl Zeiss Jenner, 8×42. The leather case and the little white bag of hydroscopic crystals are long gone. They are now my back-up pair.

There's no clock to watch, but nature is there to help relieve the tedium. Perched boldly on a small, upturned wooden crate, an inquisitive robin waits for a worm. A delicate bird, unafraid and alert, always with one eye on me, she lingers to see what's on offer.

A quarrel of house sparrows noisily squabble while nibbling on the frayed tops of a recently cut hedge. The leading male decides to raid another stretch of fresh foliage. The rest dutifully follow.

A song thrush proudly perches atop a telegraph pole and belts out his complicated melodic song. A song of many phrases, rarely repeated. His perch is well chosen. He can be heard for miles, tempting any females to take a closer look: 'Boy, can I serenade you ladies out there, wherever you are?'

A dunnock trills his gentle song from the cover of a nearby bramble thicket before retiring to the dirt floor for a snack of small spiders. This beautiful little brown bird, with a charcoal-black, pencil-fine beak, looks at me intently, eyeing me up. Whilst I remain seated she places me low down in her hierarchy of dangers.

Autumn

The autumnal equinox brings change in both weather and birds. It is still mild when the mid-September storms arrive. Sea spray is carried inland by the fierce rip on tumbling, threatening, mud-coloured breakers. A few painful flesh cuts are irritated by airborne salt, and cracked lips sting. Fine sand grains, igneous rock from a previous epoch, find ever different ways into clothes, boots and hair, never missing an opportunity to enliven a damp sandwich.

On these vast sandbanks of the shore, an ebbing tide retreats to the horizon in what seems to be a matter of minutes. The vastness of the mud banks plays games with perspective and distance: a silhouetted gull becomes an eagle, a small lone jackdaw becomes a raven. A walk out on the huge sandbank, known as Mockbeggar Wharf, disorients and is to be avoided. The soft sand and mud mixture can suck and claw at your boots like quicksand.

Having rested for several hours, the ocean returns at the alarming speed of a brisk walk. Favourite channels are first to fill before they too overflow. A determined, lazy world of foam bubbles and tiny detritus floods inexorably on. Tide on the rise drifts, glides and slides, quickly filling shallow channels, spillways and washes.

Eventually, as the tide reaches its twice-daily zenith, the strand line is reinforced with floating debris of driftwood, mermaid's purse and long, olive-green ribbons of worn kelp, their holdfasts detached in previous storms.

We are birding apprentices learning our craft. Bob leads the way when it comes to sketching the birds we see. He makes it look so easy. He shows me how to magic a bird's outline from several oval shapes, and then render in detail. What shape the forehead (steep or flat); any eye-stripes; any wing bars; any significant colours? Long legs or short? What colour the legs? What colour the rump and nape? Note down calls; these can be crucial identifiers. Any unusual habits. And then there's the 'jizz'; an ornithologist's name for the immediate impression of a bird.

Early fieldcraft skills are slowly honed here at Leasowe shore. Binoculars help, but there is nothing to beat just sitting and waiting, preferably half-hidden in warm waterproof clothes of dark greens and browns. Waiting with optimism works best. Optimism always trumps patience.

We favour a part of the sandhills near where the embankment has collapsed. We can rest almost upright, our backs supported by a dune. Thirty feet away is the latest tidal line of freshly deposited seaweed debris, mostly decomposed, covered in attendant sand flies. The tide is on the flow. We make ourselves comfortable and wait. Larger birds like oystercatcher and curlew fly directly over our heads, making for the meadows to feed. Most small wading birds feed at the tide's margin. (*Photo 4*)

Old English has their name as 'sand-yrdling' or 'sand ploughman'. A group of three sanderling feed together in the soft early morning light, just where the tide's limit refreshes the sharp shell sand. (*Photo 5*)

Air bubbles burst as dissipated backwash ripples leave tiny, stranded food morsels. Spindly legs and spurless feet run like clockwork automata; no hind claws to slow them down. The shore's precious jewels. Identical glazed porcelain pieces in their winter garb of shining whites and greys.

Sanderling feed constantly, heads down, their beaks making minute furrows in the sand. One of them regurgitates a tiny pellet. Once the tide has receded and the sanderling have moved on, Roy looks for the pellet and, to his surprise, finds it: compacted tiny fragments of mollusc and crustacean shells shaped by an invisible glue into a tiny ball.

In the northern hemisphere's early autumn these tiny birds disperse from their Arctic tundra breeding grounds, to be found weeks later on many beaches around the world, having flown non-stop for three to four days. It's been suggested that this is equivalent to a human running a continuous four-minute mile for 60 hours. I'm not sure exactly what to make of this comparison. What exactly does it tell me?

The sanderlings we see are probably having a refuelling pit stop on their autumn migration. Their journeys originate as far away as Greenland, and their final destinations will be any suitable coastline in Europe, most likely France and Spain. Alternatively, the birds on our shore at Leasowe during the summer months could well be young, sexually immature non-breeders. It makes sense for them to stay on their wintering grounds, if food is available, through their first summers whilst they are still immature; energy is saved by avoiding long, dangerous and unproductive trips to their tundra birthplace.

From autumn through winter this part of the north Wirral coast is home to large, mixed flocks of sanderling, knot and dunlin; another pair of Arctic breeders, with similar plumage differences. In summer the upper body feather colours of russet browns provide camouflage in tundra grasslands when these birds are sitting on their ground nests, hiding from local overhead raptors and ground predators such as foxes. In winter these birds lose their bright breeding colours and revert to greys, blacks and whites, more in keeping with winter's frost and snow.

We walk the line of washed-up rotting kelp and wrack. A 15-strong flock of sanderling suddenly ups sticks, for no reason we can detect, and flies erratically out to sea for 100 zig-zag yards, staying close to the surface before returning to a spot just 10 yards further up the shore. What collective decision-making is going on here? Is there an alpha male ploughman dictating play? Have they harrowed up all the food on this stretch of shore?

The flock tightens, the birds' flight pattern even more erratic. A slight panic sets in.

'Up there.'

Mac spots a peregrine falcon riding the high winds. The flock has seen her. She stoops low and one sanderling dives into the water to escape the clutches of the beautiful falcon. She climbs and nonchalantly continues her shore patrol.

The small sanderling flock go about their feeding a split second after the peregrine's killer swoop. As if nothing has happened. The danger has passed. Life continues as normal.

Earlier that week we witnessed a similar event. A sparrowhawk attacked a flock of goldfinches. The hawk surprised the charm, took an immature finch and flew to a favourite fence post to eat the bird. The rest of the flock returned to feed on nearby thistle seeds.

How much of the goldfinch behaviour is conditioned, like Pavlov's dogs? Or do these passerines only live in the present? Instinct, learned behaviour, now ingrained, tells them to be wary of the hawk or the falcon but once the danger is gone to carry on as before. Did the goldfinches know the sparrowhawk was no threat whilst it was eating nearby, albeit eating one of their own?

Just how does time work for these tiny birds? Is it all present, the 'now'? Our human observation suggests that once the immediate past is gone it carries little or no importance to the bird. But *Homo sapiens* has a sophisticated memory, and therein lies our trap. Can we apply human traits to the bird world? Just how much memory do these birds have?

Sanderlings are left to forage the strand line. Nearby in the green meadow, a fresh corpse of a young rabbit grabs our attention. Other young rabbits, presumably from the same warren, play chase. They scamper around, and at times jump over the deceased; no attempt to steer clear of the kit's fresh carcass.

WINTER

Dawn is around eight on a chosen Sunday morning in November. Soft pink light arrives slowly. Through the wet lanes and onto the dunes. A small flock of calling finches. Not our normal fare of linnets, goldfinches and greenfinches. This collection offers glimpses of white before their undulating flight takes them over the next dune.

Not for the first time, Mac is the first to identify a new bird. 'Snow buntings?' he says in his modest way. Whenever we set off for our patch, we are hopeful of spotting a rare bird. Here we have a flock!

We creep up the side of the dune and examine the scrape ahead. Using marram grass as cover and keeping breathlessly still, we look down. Yes, snow buntings! Uncommon winter visitors, and here they are, in number, on our own private patch: 14 birds feeding on wind-cleared scrapes between the dunes. Most of the birds are looking for seeds, but there is always one alert bird, a sentry with head up watching for danger and ready to raise the alarm. A couple of buntings feed on the seed heads of nearby wild grass stems. (*Photos 6 and 7*)

Snow buntings have evolved a plumage of white to survive, camou-flaged, high up above the snowline where they breed. Like sanderlings on our shore, these birds also breed in the Arctic tundra, and have a liking for estuaries, and a serious penchant for sand dunes. Although they are beautiful in their winter plumage of soft browns and white, their summer wardrobe is exquisite. The male in particular takes on a predominantly white plumage; only his back and wings are a dark chocolate brown. Black legs have white-feathered leggings, or tarsi, to help them survive in the harsh cold of the breeding grounds. They nest all around the 360 degrees of the Arctic Circle, but there are small, isolated non-Arctic breeding populations on a few mountain tops, including the Cairngorms.

As soon as the male snow bunting reaches the tundra's breeding ground he starts to sing to attract a female. He often trills in flight, but mostly when perched on a prominent spot, for all the world to admire. Females are listening for those birds who sing most. Why? A female snow bunting relies exclusively on her monogamous male partner to feed her during incubation, as it's too cold for her to leave the eggs. So she needs to pick a male who can bring in the goods. The male who sings the most must be better fed than other males, as he has more time to sing.

When north winds blow, winter days are clear and cold. Out to sea little moves. Visibility improves and distances appear to stretch. Frost covers the low-lying meadows, and dunes provide a shield from biting winds. Rivulets ice over, ponds freeze. Robins, wrens and dunnocks potter in the lane's undergrowth, and the world of nature settles down into slower, dragging rhythms. There's music in these seasons.

The strand line after a winter storm usually carries a bird corpse. Today's tribute is an emaciated oystercatcher carcass without a leg ring. Strand lines attract peregrines, kestrels and occasional sparrowhawks on their daily patrols. We see nature at work. She seems brutal and callous in our human world, which prizes empathy and compassion.

A change in wind direction to westerly brings warmer temperatures but plenty of moisture – very wet moisture. Dull grey clouds drift in from the west like conveyor belts of dirty washing. Sunken parts of meadows flood, ditches brim with rain runoff, dunes lie sodden under these overbearing skies. There is more activity in the lanes as continental redwing and fieldfare join the local blackbird population to strip berries from rowan and hawthorn. Pastures are soft enough for groups of oystercatchers to prod for worms and other invertebrates. (*Photos 8 and* 9)

Our patch is meagre and modest. We have come to know it well, like a second home. Every dried-up puddle, every wrinkle in the dunes, every fence post, every dank ditch. Lanes, tracks, paths and waterways have their own two-word nicknames: withy path, ragwort pasture, arrowe brook, daisy bank, higher dune, rabbit track and chiffie sedge. A quick and easy personal guide to use when we chat over a day's notes and recollections.

We set off with a reasonable idea of what we might find: blue tits in the hawthorn, oystercatchers on the pastures, sanderling on the tide line. But we hope for the atypical. The trek is made in the hope of the unexpected. What might be in the horse paddock today? What might daisy bank offer at the afternoon's high tide at 2.30 pm? Has that couple of purple sandpipers stuck around the crumbled embankment's rockslide? We know the tranquil shadows where nature hides.

The probable normal is silently acknowledged; we make time for the possibly unusual.

There are times when a few close shaves make us think on. There are serious consequences to a misjudged tide out on the bank. A misread storm can easily strand us without shelter. When young heads do finally hit the bedtime pillow, rerun scenes of a day's highlights bring warm feelings of achievement. Shared fears and confidences bring a tightness to our little band.

The satisfied sleep of the happily weary.

Glimpses of different understandings, different loyalties, worlds away from the fixed, given template that is family and home. Loyalties are now shared with the group. Time with mates matters. The group has priority over the individual. We belong. We share secrets. A singularly formative time in our young lives. But that's hindsight for you.

3

RODS AND CONES

Spring arrives in late March, and a few (Eurasian) blue tits display smarter, brighter plumages. In good light, dazzling spring colours of sea and sand; azure blue uppers and bright daffodil yellow underparts. Comical face patterns with white cheek patches bordered in black, and a narrow black eye-stripe, as if the little bird has just unsuspectingly worn a pair of joke-shop ink-staining goggles. Dark long spindly legs and surprisingly long claws for its diminutive size grip at every angle in the upper branches of the hawthorn hedge along the narrow path. Constantly calling to each other to keep in group contact, high-pitched 'sisisi' or their more assertive 'tsek, tsek!' if there's any danger to the group. A robin shares the hawthorn's lower branches and looks up to the skies when the tits give their alarm call. Has the robin recognised the alarm call as well?

My notebook entry for the day asks the question 'Do some blue tits have richer, more intensely coloured blue caps than others?' Is this their own, homegrown sapphire crown? I read in a library book that female blue tits prefer males with brighter, more intense blue caps. Gosh, my little observation has merit. A confidence builder. An encouragement to make a few more notes and observations when I'm out next time.

It turns out the males are posing: 'Look at my lovely blue cap, you ladies.'

Come to think of it, Dad wears a fine trilby on his way to work. Other guys on the estate prefer flat caps. I'm not sure, though, if Dad's trilby has quite the same pulling magic as the blue tit's azure cap. If it does, he keeps it to himself. I guess it makes him feel good. He went bald as a young man.

Science tells us that blue tits have a retina which detects light in the ultraviolet, and as a result their azure blue cap has an intensity we can't appreciate. A female blue tit is exquisitely aware, turned on even, by his dazzling diadem.

As they can see wavelengths of light that we can't, this begs a big question: Who are we to say that what we see is all there is to see, and who are we to say that our version of the world is the only one that matters? It helps to understand the science involved. Put simply, sight is the ability of our brains to turn electromagnetic radiation, in this case light, into images from which we can derive meaning.

Just what is electromagnetic radiation? For our purposes, it emanates from our sun, the big bright star in our sky. A nuclear furnace burning fuel and giving off ginormous amounts of energy in the form of electromagnetic radiation.[12]

Science – the same science which provides quality medical care, gets us to the moon, builds skyscrapers, manufactures smartphones, televisions, cars and so on – tells us[13] that we humans see in only a specific band of light wavelengths. This band of wavelengths is what we quite naturally call the visible light spectrum. Perhaps we should rename this range of wavelengths 'the *Homo sapiens* visible light spectrum', as we are not capable of interpreting the light wavelengths, ultraviolet and infrared, at either end of our visible light spectrum.

Sight is the result of photons of light detected on our retina, at the back of the eye, by an array of tiny structures called rods and cones. Cones detect the wavelengths, or colours, and rods detect the intensity, the energy, of light. Most humans have three types of cone to detect the three primary colours: blue, green and red. Our brains, fully enclosed in a dark, lightless cranium, mix the three colours to provide the complete

---

12 Electromagnetic radiation has wave properties, but it is also described in terms of a stream of extremely high-energy, massless particles, photons, each travelling in a wave-like pattern at the speed of light. Photons have no mass and are all energy. Each photon contains a certain amount of energy. The different types of radiation are defined by the amount of energy found in the photons: radio waves have photons with low energies, microwave photons have more energy than radio-wave photons, infrared photons have still more, then visible light, ultraviolet light, X-rays, and the most energetic of all, gamma-ray photons.

13 'Evidence-based' is the politician's currently over-borrowed rhetoric.

visible spectrum – but birds, like our blue tits, have evolved a fourth cone type, which detects ultraviolet light.

So their view of the world is, in their own unique way, enhanced over ours. There are many other examples where birds have vision capabilities we don't have. Eagles and other raptors have evolved the ability to see prey at great distance and in fine detail: they have four times as many cones and rods per square millimetre of retina than us humans. Their eyeballs are more elliptical in shape, inherited from their distant reptile ancestors, offering natural telephoto properties. When I'm walking in the high sierras looking for eagles, I am only too aware that any bird in the area will have seen me long before I clock them, such is their different eyesight.

A fellow bird photographer has scary proof of an eagle's incredible eyesight. He wanted to take shots of a pair of golden eagles. He trekked in the Cairngorms in April to a spot near an eyrie, knowing the parent birds would be feeding at least one young eaglet, possibly two. He found a gully where he could hide. He chose a spot which was under the eagles' normal flight path to and from the eyrie, 400 yards away. He was close to the eyrie, but not so close, he judged, that he would cause any disturbance. He arrived at dawn and settled down for the day. He made sure, of course, that both he and his camera were suitably camouflaged. He even wore a black balaclava to hide his face, convinced that the only part of his body visible to the eagles would be his eyes.

Both parent birds were feeding their young. Every time one of them flew by they took an interest in the spot where he lay. The male eagle, slightly smaller, was having none of it. On his third pass he circled above him for several minutes, getting lower and lower, dropping 100 feet to take a closer look: typical behaviour before a kill or to inspect carrion. The photographer was convinced this eagle had spotted him as a lunch prospect, noticing the eyeholes in the balaclava, and was intent on working out if he was prey or not. 'I got a few good shots, but it was pretty scary.'

Nocturnal birds similarly out-see humans in the dark. Owls have more need of light than colour to hunt at night, and evolution's solution is a retina with more rods than cones. More rods per square millimetre of retina make better use of every photon available and as a result their prey is more discernible in the dark.

What about infrared, at the other end of the human visible light spectrum? Many of us are familiar with television images provided by infrared cameras which detect heat, often body heat. Heat, be it from a living being or from a poorly insulated roof, is a transmitter of infrared electromagnetic radiation. It turns out that many animals can detect infrared. Snakes use a row of pits along their jaws to detect infrared heat rays, and use these detectors to build up a picture of their prey in what to us is total darkness.

The Arctic caribou has been around for over 1.6 million years, says the fossil record from the Yukon. On the face of it this is not a highly evolved species, but research by a team from University College London in 2012 has shown that the eyes of an Arctic caribou detect light at the ultraviolet wavelength. Why would that specific ability be of evolutionary value? Well, the caribou's greatest predator threat is wolves, which for their own survival have adapted to the snowscape by evolving white and grey coats. The caribou, thanks to their ultraviolet vision, see body heat from wolves as almost black, visible for miles.

The caribou is but one of an estimated 1 to 2 million species of animals on our planet. Evolution has endowed each species with a uniquely different way of seeing the world. Each unique view has evolved for individual species, enhancing its chances of survival in its own environment.

We humans can't see in the ultraviolet because of the compromises made as we evolved. We have limited brain capacity due to the size of our skull, and evolution has decided that detecting ultraviolet light does not have sufficient survival benefits when compared with other more advantageous developments, such as sophisticated language. As *Homo sapiens* moved to more temperate climates, so we evolved less body hair and lighter skin. Lighter-skinned *Homines sapientes* are more prone to the damaging effects of excessive exposure to ultraviolet light. We have evolved to the point where we have ultraviolet filters in the lenses of our eyes, because these rays – the main cause of melanoma skin cancers – are very harmful to us. Excessive exposure to prolonged ultraviolet radiation causes corneal damage, cataracts and macular degeneration.

At the age of 66, after years of walking in open spaces without sunglasses, this *Homo sapiens* had both cataracts removed. A cataract is simply a defective, damaged lens. The slow deterioration in the lens leads to its increasing opaqueness as well as the loss of its ability to focus. Over time, the lens becomes cloudy, and what light does get through takes on a dull, yellowy-brown milky hue, which we get used to. If left to its own devices, the lens becomes so cloudy that light cannot penetrate and we go blind. Fortunately, the cataract procedure is quite straightforward. It involves removing the damaged lens with a narrow beam of ultrasound. The sonic wave breaks up the defective lens, the bits are extracted and then a small immaculately made, lens is inserted – glued – in place.

The bandage was taken off after 24 hours and like everyone else, after this 30-minute procedure, I was blown away by the new bright, blueish-tinged, white light. So different from the dull yellows to which you grow accustomed. To celebrate my new, bright, bluish-white sight I sat under the cover of a rowan tree in Ynys-hir RSPB reserve near Machynlleth, marvelling at my new vision. I saw once again the crisp bright outlines of yellowy-green willow warblers taking their lunch in the light green canopy. Was I really seeing shades of lime and shamrock greens up there? Welcome back to the world of nature again. I stayed under the tree for over two hours humbly appreciating my new sight, my new reality.

Later that evening, over a pint, I mentioned to a few friends my time at Ynys-hir and my new eyesight. One of them, in his well-meaning way, suggested that my new sight was a miracle. I tried ever so gently to point out it is medical science that has provided me with decent sight, after his Great Designer had seen fit to allow my eyes to degenerate into near-blindness. Perhaps I was being a little harsh?

During that time under the rowan watching those willow warblers I wondered yet again just what were they seeing. How is their world enhanced by ultraviolet vision? A young rabbit slowly shuffled its way into the nearby nettles. How does this animal see the world? How is its reality different from mine? This quest has stuck with me for some time. It is a world of ideas which can carry many metaphysical[14] concepts, such as the meaning of existence, the concept of a soul, what happened before the big bang, and what do we mean by 'causality'? This is a world that can be viewed either under the scrutiny of the philoso-

---

14   The word 'metaphysics' comes from the Greek for 'after physics'. Metaphysical ideas are
     not based on either direct observation or measurement of the world around us.

pher's metaphysical reason and logic or informed by the scriptures of various religions. If we limit our perceptions to those two disciplines, which is it to be?

As a younger man I was overwhelmed by the aura around the words 'metaphysics' and 'philosopher'. These were words from a world beyond my grasp – a world seen briefly when the likes of A.J. Ayers, Jacob Bronowski and others appeared on the small tv tube in BBC's *The Brains Trust*. These were fascinating, pre-eminent wise men.

As an older man I tell myself that perhaps these intellectuals are not completely outside my reach. After all a philosopher is simply a lover of wisdom. Several years ago I read Kant's assertion to the effect that new knowledge is at first perceived by our senses, then comes our understanding of it, and eventually it is our reason that completes the process; that assertion has stuck with me.

We can be sure that our own version of the world is not the only version. That we are the apex predator on our planet does not, despite the protestations of some unenlightened beings, carry with it the notion we are divinely, inherently superior. Evolution has equipped all sentient beings to sense the world in different ways to suit different conscious needs. Our cognitive abilities are different, not necessarily superior. Evolution has no grand plan.

'Are we to believe our senses?' is a fundamental question when it comes to understanding nature. If our ideas of nature depend on what our senses tell us, then how can we be sure that what we sense in our mind is out there? Early Greek philosophers pondered these empirical questions. Among them was Democritus (460–370 BCE).[15] He was sceptical of sense data, and introduced the idea of secondary qualities. He thought things like colour, sound and taste are more in our mind than in the thing itself. He also said that sensations are atoms falling on sense organs, and that all senses are essentially forms of touch.

For Democritus to suggest that colour was in the mind and not a real thing 'of itself' was quite extraordinary. He was right – but proof of this did not come until 2,000 years later, when Newton offered us his insight

---

15 Democritus was certainly my kind of guy, as he questioned all received wisdoms. He did not believe in gods or an afterlife. He is called 'the laughing philosopher' because he found life much more cheerful without what he considered to be the depressing superstitions of religion.

that white light is a collection of all colours of the rainbow. Light can be split into its component colours by passing a beam through a prism.

Colour is an example of how our senses interpret the real world. When white light shines on an object some colours bounce off the object and others are absorbed by it. Our eyes see only those colours, or wavelengths, which are reflected. A red ball, or a robin's breast for that matter, is not red intrinsically or 'of itself'. It is simply a material whose pigment absorbs all colour wavelengths but that of red. And then it is our brain which forms the picture of the real world as we understand it, as soon as those photons, discrete balls of massless energy, hit our rods and cones.

To put Democritus's thoughts into context we must remember that at his time, and indeed for many centuries later, the brain was thought to be a muscle which helped cool the body. Nobody knew where the mind lay. Indeed, the mind was thought to have an independent existence outside the body. This view persists to the present day, of course, amongst some of those of a religious persuasion, who believe in the soul. However some religious folk are happy to equate the brain with the mind but still see the soul as existing outside the body.

4

MOCKBEGGAR WHARF AND HOYLE BANK

It is noon on Boxing Day 1962, when large, dense snowflakes gently fall, hanging in the cold air. Within an hour our empty street is littered in deep snow: a good 4 inches. Visibility is just a few yards in the dim light of late afternoon.

The weather forecast on the wireless suggests this weather is here for the week: a slow-moving warm front from the Atlantic is hitting a stationary high-pressure system over Iceland, which is bringing cold air down from the Arctic. We lock up for the night.

My first waking thought is to look outside and check the snow is still there. The sun is a hazy orange ball low to the east. A few indolent snow clouds appear above terrace roofs, but the new untroubled blanket white snowfall is intact, pristine even, stretching what little light there is.

What will be different in our patch up at the shore? I have no understanding of what snow does to the world of nature. Perhaps nothing will have changed overnight; perhaps everything.

The side roads have few imprints, human or animal. The long, straight main road is free of traffic, the dense hedgerows on the far side topped with several inches of snow. The large oak which stands upright, sentry-like, next to the red-brick church has its own skeletal covering. As if the upper surface of every bough has been painstakingly sprayed with a layer of white icing sugar, a good inch deep. The illusion is corrupted when a sudden gust blows loose powdered snow from the oak's limbs, falling as several white transparent veils, wafted, one could believe, by playful dryads.

All is still again. The only sound is the regular crunch of compacted snow under my boots.

The snow cover on the main road is scarred by a few cars carefully following the deep tracks of their predecessors. Straight-line tyre trails emphasise a geometry of perspective and distance. The main road has long linear grooves in the packed snow, both right and left, which converge to single points. Dots without depth. Distance is flat as snow seems to eliminate a dimension, and without a blue sky there is little contrast.

The gap in the hedge leading to the path is framed for the first time in a white architrave. The gravel on the narrow lane to the shore is covered in several inches, deeper in places where finger drifts have formed from gaps in the hedge. I expect more animal and bird tracks. Perhaps these fresh prints, near my feet, are those of a wandering, bemused fox. Snow is still falling, and my own embossed wellington boot prints are soon covered, cancelling out my tracks, my visit.

Virgin snow lies deep in ragwort pasture. Picking out the path is an act of memory. Head for the gap in the fence. Sandhills are eerily serene as nature's sounds are dampened. The dunes have their own sculpted windblown crusts where powdered snow has hardened on the leeward side of many ridges. Fresh snowfalls stick to damp tidal sands, only to be washed away by an incoming, dissolving ripple.

Food is still available. A nutritious haven hidden under white wrapping. Busy blackbirds search in clumps of sweet grass where gusts have cleared snow from areas of meadowland. Blue tits call out their urgent, musical rasps, high in hawthorn. Finches flock and thrushes fly high. Redshank in frozen snow scour the mudflats for morsels. (*Photo 10*)

A week goes by; there is no let-up. Snow upon snow. Layered, compacted strata drape main roads, making motorised travel slow and difficult. Ungritted roads are empty. Lanes used by tractors form icy, corrugated surfaces like a heavy-duty corduroy. Strong winds over higher ground bring extensive drifts resembling enormous soft pillows. Many roads and railway lines are blocked. Trains must be dug out by gangs with shovels. Nights are extremely cold, well below freezing. Overnight hoar frosts form cornflake-like crusts over soft snow: brittle shells, which crack like thin, frozen cardboard.

After weeks of below-zero temperatures, ferry boats in the Mersey plough their way through inches of frozen, sloshing sea ice. High tide at Leasowe brings in buckled ice crystals, a few the size of large boulders slush in the slow floe. The sea is placid with its ice burden. As the tide recedes, jagged shards of thin patterned sheet ice are left beached.

Birding is difficult. The ground is frozen, nothing gives. The giant outline of a few oak and elm appear gaunt, lifeless. A short stretch of evergreen laurel hedge stands testament to a long-off spring. Tall, desiccated grass stems crack and break like dead twigs. Deep drains and gullies are frozen solid. High in the dunes, marram grasses, festooned with flickering icicles, stand neutered in freezing air. The once fecund land is cruelly impotent.

A desolate landscape made more shocking by the strange, relentless longevity of the big freeze. Nothing moves in this sterile world. A frigid calm descends as the cold, still air from the Arctic settles like a heavy, wrinkled shroud. Winter is deep in icy ground. Cold grips the soil miserly tight in her clutch. Exhaled breath immediately condenses into to a faint smoky-grey transient trace.

Where are those warm westerlies when you need them? Each new dawn offers the possibility of a thaw, but every morning's new thin pale light throws the same dull shadows on frozen compacted footpaths, iced ditches and bare thorny hedgerows. Nothing changes. The soft wintry sun of mid-day has no warmth, no energy to melt and unlock. Apart from an occasional snow shower the days are stubbornly grim, well below zero. Brutal, remorseless cold grinds on for all of January and then all of February.

On and on and on.

Birds have moved from our patch. An empty, sterile landscape proffers few opportunities to nourish and nurture, sustain and support. Dead birds wash up on the shore; emaciated carcasses offer scant nutrients to scrawny scavenging gulls.

At low tide a picayune wader searches in hope of a morsel. A robin scuttles in fractured undergrowth. All is locked down. No respite. The world of nature can be stubborn.

The only hope is the certainty of spring. A day in early March brings a few minutes of brittle warmth at midday. Nothing melts, but there's a hint of a thaw to come. The next day's temperature pattern repeats, but the minutes of a lazy cool sun extend to an hour. What little snow melts forms pools which overnight freeze into a layer of blue ice. Dustings of powdered snow on these hidden surfaces make them treacherous. After my first fall I take extra care.

By mid-March the snow is all but gone, but favourite haunts are eerily empty. The narrow, straight path first trod the morning after the first fall, way back on Boxing Day, has eventually lost its snow cover apart from a few isolated footprints of compressed ice made ten weeks ago by my wellington boots.

There are no bird voices to break the dull, grey silence. The big freeze has taken its toll. It may be a few years before bird numbers are back to normal, if ever they recover.

Spring is near when a late morning's gentle warmth lasts into mid-afternoon. Trickles of running water appear from beneath remaining snowdrifts, now littered with a crust of sooty blown dirt. Miniature green buds on hawthorn and blackthorn offer hope. A few newly arrived house martins swoop for insects in the sandhills, and meadow pipits take up territories along the embankment. But where there should be 20 pairs we find just a couple.

A lone skylark takes off and climbs vertically into the blue sky with his heavenly song. 'Ethereal minstrel! pilgrim of the sky!'[16] He's calling to his mate on the ground as she broods her clutch of four mottled brown eggs, hidden in her nest of concealed coiled grass. (*Photo 11*)

The western horizon from Leasowe is dominated by the whitewashed Leasowe lighthouse. The distant beacon stands ghostly proud above low-lying early morning mist. It's a 30-minute walk from our sandhills, but there's no easy, direct path.

There is a passable route to Moreton at low tide, along the shoreline, where 20-foot cliffs, damaged by storms, are slowly eroding. Bold trespass on the private golf course behind these cliffs provides an alternative route. The market gardeners have stories that the golf course was once a famous horse racing venue, stretching along this section of shoreline

---

16   William Wordsworth, 'To the skylark', 1825.

from Leasowe as far as Wallasey:[17] 'You can't miss the octagonal tower, where they watched the races from, part of old Mockbeggar Hall. The old light is another half a mile or so.'

The walk is possible at low tide along the base of the crumpled cliff, once protected by a concrete embankment. The remnants are now strewn around the bay in lumps of rubble, some the size of a small car. Mac leads the way as we dodge the scattered debris of a rock-strewn shoreline and scramble up a loose incline. Sure enough, there across the narrow fairway an octagonal tower stands proud above the rooflines of a collection of newer buildings, now a convalescent home for those who worked the railways.

A few oystercatchers probe the green turf, but Roy spots a busy male stonechat displaying to an attendant female. The bird strikes a proud pose atop a gorse in full yellow bloom, flitting from perch to perch in the upper echelons of the gorse but finally settling for a fence post. His black head, like a hood, extends down to his chin and nape. The white around the side of the neck emphasises his dark cowl. His orange-red breast and flecked brown back add to his charisma. His name reflects his call, like two stones knocked together, repetitive but with an enquiring assertion, as if to say to the listening female, 'Did you hear that? Not bad, eh?' The nearby female, in her duller plumage, pays little attention and keeps a low profile in the bracken. She's not yet convinced. (*Photos 12 and 13*)

On the shore a turnstone squeals an alarm call. At low tide, there's a path out of this little bay up to the ribbon of embankment which has survived the storms. In the near distance, the lighthouse sits in its place, set back a good 100 yards from the shore.

The embankment overlooks reclaimed land, now a low open meadow. No market gardens or golf courses here. This is common land, a few feet below the sea level of a high tide: Moreton Common, where on balmy

---

17 We know that horse racing was a popular local activity in Leasowe in 16th and 17th centuries. It is thought the first building here, an octagonal tower, may have been used to watch this sporting spectacle. The old racecourse is now a golf course. We also know these horse races were the forerunner to the Derby races, reflecting the strong probability that the original Leasowe Castle was built for Ferdinando Stanley, 5th Earl of Derby. It was Ferdinando's brother William, the 6th Earl, described as a noted sportsman, who is remembered as a keen supporter of the Wallasey (Leasowe) races. By 1700 this tower was derelict, but other buildings had been added. It became known as Mockbeggar Hall long before it became a hotel.

summer days yellow box-kites are flown, dogs are walked, balls are kicked and picnics consumed. Moreton Common is a bit of a local tourist spot in high summer.[18]

Leasowe lighthouse is a short walk from the common; it lies empty, locked, derelict and technically in Moreton. Rumour has its foundations were made from cotton bales washed up from a shipwreck. Built in 1763 from 660,000 hand-made bricks. The Liverpool Corporation Docks Committee was keen to improve access to its thriving new docks, and the lighthouse marked the entrance to Rock Channel, the deep water entrance to the Mersey. The last light shone in 1908. The Rock Channel had silted, no longer navigable. The lighthouse became redundant.

Up close, the lighthouse loses the some of the allure its distance had offered. The whitewash is fading and dirty, but the lines and diminishing curves of its meticulous brickwork still enchant. (*Photos 14 and 15*)

Time is on our side. We decide to follow the embankment further west towards Meols, the next village along the shoreline.

The name 'Meols' harks back to an old Norse term for sandbanks. The two villages of Meols and Hoylake are connected by another concrete embankment built in the 1890s by the local authorities as the first sea wall. Most of the land here is at, or just below, sea level. The north Wirral coastline was rapidly eroding at the end of the 19th century, due in part to dredging operations in the River Mersey to accommodate growing numbers of bigger ships into the new, major port of Liverpool. The concrete embankment saved the coastline, but the sea wall changed local currents, and valuable archaeological sites at Meols were buried in sand, thankfully not before many artefacts were collected. Finds accumulated date back to pre-Roman Carthage, the Roman Empire and, more recently, those pesky marauding Vikings. Wirral is replete with place names left by the men from the North. These finds point unequivocally to Meols being a major seaport at the time. Geography supports this conclusion.

There is a coastal location beside Meols called the Hoyle Lake, with a depth of 5 fathoms at low tide, a natural harbour on the Irish Sea coast. The excavated objects found, now on display at six institutions in the

---

18   The railway line under the Mersey from Liverpool stops at Leasowe and Moreton, and visitors come in their thousands for a day out. My lovely gran used to look after kids who got lost when the place was busy. She had a small wooden hut, and any lost kids would be taken to her to be looked after until claimed by anxious parents.

north-west of England including the Museum of Liverpool, show that the port began to develop 2,400 years ago, during the Iron Age.

A coin – a silver tetradrachan from Syria, minted in the 1st century BCE – some Romano-British brooches, and some bronze coins of the Roman Emperor Augustus, as well as some Viking weaponry, medieval buckles and dress fittings, were also uncovered along this part of the north Wirral shore as soil erosion took its course.[19]

At Dove Point in Meols a groyne of heavy boulders runs out to sea for 100 yards, built to help stop the movement of sediment by strong tides, known as longshore drift. A good birding spot? Worth a detour? Our reward is a neat collection of waders. At the far tip, redshank, turnstone, oystercatcher, dunlin and curlew take a snooze, their heads tucked neatly under their wings. All face into wind.

Out to sea a group of seven cormorants file past with their ungainly but effective mechanical flight: heads and neck stretched, regular, deliberate wing beats, straight flight lines and no fuss. One by one, calling curlews leave the safety of their roost and fly back over our heads towards the damp, nourishing brooks and drained marshes of Moreton's carrs.

Time to take stock. The tide is in, the wind keen. In these rough sea conditions birds who would normally migrate down the middle of a relatively calm Irish Sea seek the shelter of less ferocious conditions near the coast.

'Ideal time for a sea watch?' says Mac.

Make yourself comfortable, use the slope of the embankment, wrap up in several layers, hold your bins so your elbows take the weight on your chest. Rucksacks make a worthy head rest. Late spring storms can produce sightings of terns, sea ducks, gulls, divers, petrels and shearwaters as well as arriving winter waders.

If one of us sees anything unusual it's crucial we tell each other immediately where it is, out there in the cold grey-green seascape.

'Ten past, halfway out, going left, alone,' is a typical shout.

Another pair of eyes can corroborate, add more detail, but typically 20 seconds is the time we have a bird in view. We have an idea what the

---

19   Finds from Meols have been published in a monograph: Griffiths, D. et al. (2007) 'Meols: The Archaeology of the North Wirral Coast'. Oxford University School of Archaeology: monograph 68.

bird might be, as in effect there are just a few birds it could be, but if the sighting is new to any of us then it needs written notes. Often this is a full page in our black notebooks; not the dismissive one-line entry for the often seen. A chance to start to practise scientific objectivity.

This is Roy's domain: 'Just write down in yer notebook what you see.'

Easy words. Not so easy when it's cold and raining, the late afternoon light is poor, the bird is flying past at speed, low down, and the sea's swell often hides the thing. Its plumage is nondescript and well-worn after a successful breeding summer. Just how big is it? Is it near or far? Do we have other birds in view to compare size? Descriptive data must be reliable. A primitive sketch is even better. Bob's sketches are not primitive; more like the work of an accomplished illustrator.

Good practice dictates we should only refer to our reference books when notes are complete, shared and agreed. After all we don't want to unconsciously influence our jottings, do we? That's the theory. In practice we dive headlong into our *Collins Field Guide*. When we do see an unusual bird, our collective, agreed notes, together with any sketches, are sent off to a local identification committee. On the rare occasion we will write to God, the birding county recorder for all of Cheshire.

After an hour on the hard, cold, flat concrete, muscles are numb. Time to call it a day. Mac takes up his bins and looks at a new area of exposed shore ahead of us, dotted with low black stumps, covering a large area, possibly half a football pitch. We discover an area of dead tree-trunk stubs clearly visible as the tide recedes. We scramble over hard, coal-black, jagged butts, each no bigger than a foot diameter. This must be remnants of an old, submerged forest. We are putting our wellies down on another, long-gone, world.

The earliest mention of the submerged forest occurs in a description of Cheshire dated 1615 by William Webb, entitled Kings Vale Royal, in which he calls the forest the 'Meols Stocks', alluding to the antediluvian origins of the forest:

> In these mosses, especially in the black, are fir-trees found under the ground, in some places six feet deep or more, and in others not one foot; which trees are of surprising length, and straight, having certain small branches like boughs, and roots at one end – as if they had been

blown down by the winds; and yet no man can tell that ever any such trees did grow there, nor yet how they should come thither. Some are of the opinion that they have lain there ever since Noah's flood.

Are we treading in antiquity, tramping an old forest, once home to animals of another age? Would we have seen mammoth and great elk in these forests, in the time before the last Ice Age?

The sun is low in the late afternoon sky. Ahead of us lies yet more exploration of Hoylake and West Kirby, but not today. Our patch is growing.

We turn to walk back to Leasowe, but out to sea 30 or so large, dark birds flap their wings in regular beats – not fast, not slow, just regular. They are coming our way and look to us like buzzards, but they can't be – 30 buzzards?

'I think they're ravens,' says Mac.

'But there are loads of them, I make it 34.' Only pedants count.

Ravens normally go around in pairs. We have never seen such a spectacle. We watch in silence as the birds – all 36, I was wrong – call occasionally to each other with contact calls; several variations of a deep guttural 'cronk'.

As they arrive over our heads the entire group starts an acrobatic display of tumbles and rolls, accompanied by noisy, higher-pitched chatter.

'Blimey. Are they playing?' asks Bob.

'I think so,' says Mac. 'They could be celebrating reaching land.'

Their massive heads and beaks and bright dark shiny eyes give them an ominous look. Twenty yards in from the sea, over the pastures, the flock reforms into an orderly group for the rest of its journey. The birds continue towards a distant copse of oak and sycamore. (*Photo 16*)

'Looks as if they're going to roost,' says Mac.

'Sure does,' says Bob. 'It's that time of day. Just like us.'

'But they flew in over the sea,' I interpose. 'Where do you think they came from? Surely not all the way from Ireland.'[20]

During the walk home we chat briefly about birds playing and those ravens coming in off the sea. Mac recalls a story from the recent big freeze.

---

20   It was not until 2010 that I found out that Newborough Warren on Anglesey is the home of a large roost of over 1,000 ravens who come over from Ireland simply to spend the night in the mixed woodlands of Newborough. As members of the crow family *corvidae*, they are intelligent birds with a vocabulary of noises which they use to great effect in both family and bigger groups. Were these birds part of that evening's procession from Ireland, albeit slightly off course?

'Last winter, two carrion crows took to sliding down the snow-covered roof of the house across the road from us, on a piece of old cardboard. They must have taken at least five goes each. I can't think of any other way to describe it – they were playing and enjoying themselves.'

The conversation turns to the submerged forest. Was it really an old forest, and if so, how old? As we walk Leasowe's lanes, we ask a guy still working his market garden, weeding his leeks.

'Excuse me,' says Bob, 'we were wondering if you might be able to help us.' (He can be so polite at times.) 'Do you know anything about the submerged forest which we've just seen near Dove Point in Meols?'

'Oh, my goodness,' says the gardener, 'yes. These old forests have been covered for many years by silt, but occasionally a storm will clear loose sand and expose the old forests. There were forests all the way from Wallasey and Birkenhead to West Kirby.' He quotes a line of oral history: 'From Birkinheven [Birkenhead] unto Hilbree, a squirrel may jump from tree to tree.'

We fancy exploring the last stretch of the north Wirral coast from Meols through to Hoylake and West Kirby. Although no-one says as much, we want to check into all the birding possibilities from Leasowe to Hoylake, and we're missing a stretch. We meet at the lighthouse early on a Saturday morning on our bikes. Mine's a birthday present, a Raleigh with cool drop handlebars and Sturmey-Archer gears, the world's first three-speed internal gear hub for bicycles, and all from Nottingham. I am proud of this bike – even known to clean it, albeit very occasionally.

It's an easy ride along the lanes to Meols, past the submerged forest to the slipway at Dove Point where inshore fishing smacks and a few dinghies are launched. Further west is Hoyle Lake, a deep water channel even at low tide, stretching up to the village of the same name. It's protected by Hoyle Bank. When the tide is running it's a favourite spot for colourful shelduck flotillas to collect in small groups of five or ten, looking for tiny hydrobia snails.

We ride the road along the embankment from Meols, pass the RNLI lifeboat station and go as far as King's Gap in Hoylake,[21] where the road

---

21   By the 17th century Hoylake had become one of the main embarkation points for troops sailing to Ireland, including King William III and his army of 10,000 to fight the Battle of the Boyne in 1690 against the Roman Catholic Stuart ex-King of England, James II. The location of his departure is still known today as King's Gap. Hoylake's part in our sectarian history was commemorated by the members of the Liverpool Orange Lodge, who in 2012 paraded along the very same road on a Bank Holiday Monday. Yes, a celebration of protestant triumphalism was still deemed necessary 322 years later in a modest north Wirral town. I hope the roadworks at the time were not too much of an incumbrance for these loyal Liverpool unionists.

takes a sharp left; 100 yards on the right we look out for Stanley Road. At the end of this road is our destination. Red Rocks. A collection of red sandstone outcrops, sand dunes, marshy reedbeds and low-lying shrubs of alder and sallow. The place where the north Wirral coast does a 90-degree turn south into the Dee Estuary, and home to a local colony of natterjack toad.

In winter Red Rocks is a refuge for all those wading birds which have been feeding on the vast mudflats of the Dee Estuary and Liverpool Bay.

A single, mixed flock, numbering in the thousands, gathers here at high tide, taking a well-earned rest. The highest count, to my knowledge, here on the Dee Estuary, has been 30,000 birds. The pantry door of those massive mudflats is shut for a couple of hours until the tide recedes and their feeding grounds show again. Oystercatcher, curlew, redshank, knot, dunlin, grey plover, godwits and others jostle in what becomes a single, enormous tightly packed roost. It is thought their proximity to each other helps conserve body heat in cold winter conditions. As we've noted before, the entire flock faces into the wind.

The flock gets the jitters over a passing falcon and a section takes to the air, a writhing, contorting, mesmerising flock of up to 10,000 birds. Flashes of whites and greys. A tight interconnected flow like a generous, grey ribbon, billowing in the wind. (*Photo 17*)

A time to gape. A time to gawk.

Recent research suggests there are a few leading individuals – the alpha males perhaps – in flocks that size, but the synchronous pattern they weave is down to the ability of each bird to follow the closest birds to them, perhaps 6 or 7 individuals. A collision-free zone. Reaction times are in milliseconds – but react they do, to their immediate neighbours.

Part of the flock settles again and the rest follow suit. The roost occasionally ripples as if a transparent standing pressure wave travels through the crush. Birds bunch, surge and settle again and hide their heads under their wings. Shut-eye time.

There's safety in numbers for these wader flocks, but nevertheless they attract birds of prey, especially speedy peregrine falcons. Several birds in the roost take up lookout duty. Falcons can be spotted much earlier by a group than by an individual. We have often said that our four pairs of eyes are always better than one pair.

The attraction of this flock to the falcon is the distinct possibility that an injured bird will be amongst the throng. Peregrines have a hit rate in the region of one in ten when it comes to attacking wader flocks; they often have better chances when they target unsuspecting birds travelling alone.

A single, confident redshank takes flight, away from the throng. (*Photo 18*)

Red Rocks provides another spectacular view across the widest stretch of the Dee Estuary. In the middle of the estuary, and tantalisingly close to the Wirral shore, is Hilbre Island. In fact, there are three islands: Little Eye, Middle Hilbre and Hilbre itself. These islands are so different to the safe 5-mile stretch of embankment along the shoreline from Leasowe to Hoylake via Moreton and Meols. They offer yet another world to explore, but a world moated by high tide. So close but so different. Just how different we are yet to understand.

5

LEASOWE WRECKERS

I left Leasowe as an 18-year-old. I have been back a few times since, to visit my Ma. Today is another chance to retrace those tracks, paths, lanes and brooks. The narrow path from the main road seems narrower and smaller, but it can't be. It's no longer a frightening walk, of course. The market gardens are still there, looking scruffy but trading still. The walk to the sandhills seems shorter now. Another example of how our brains deceive us. Does youthful exuberance exaggerate distance, or does sanguine old age diminish size? Or both?

A relentless, onshore breeze cuts diagonally across ragwort pasture. A lone kestrel hovers against the wind then dips for the kill but returns unrewarded to patrol the next sector of sunken meadow. (*Photo 19*) Oystercatchers and curlew prod the turf, and crows skulk in shrubs sculpted by constant westerlies. The sense of scale might have changed, but otherwise much is as it was.

Sandhills are soon crossed. The inevitable litter competes with strands of rusted barbed wire which protrude from the dunes' mobile scrapes. A meadow pipit, with its long hind claw, preens on a weathered wooden post infested with minute snails. Right-hand-coiled exoskeleton shells make fancy patterns on a worn, moss-covered timber post.

The embankment has been renewed and improved. It is now possible to walk all the way to Moreton and beyond. Notice boards with a map and sketches of local wildlife announce I am in the North Wirral Coastal

Park. Opened in 1986 by the Metropolitan Borough of Wirral, it covers the exact area where we young lads began our birding adventures: 400 acres in total, including the shoreline from Leasowe to Meols. There's a bridleway now, and several footpaths, and of course the old lanes and streams are still there. It's also a place for the many dog walkers to enjoy the sea front.

The immodest thought struck me that perhaps our birding endeavours all those years ago first identified this stretch of coast as an important refuge for nature. Were we responsible for the initial interest? I guess we will never know for sure. It's not important. What is relevant, though, is that it's a park with an SSSI designation (Site of Special Scientific Interest) and the protection that comes with this nomination. It's a space open to the public, encompassing commonland pastures, shorelines and sandhills.

With the help of the repaired embankment, I get to the renovated lighthouse in quick time. It is now the ranger's office and information centre. Near the lighthouse there's a guy in his fifties with a pair of binoculars strung around his neck. His bins are trained on a bird on a wire. Our conversation is typical between two birders.

'Is there anything about?' I ask.

'Nothing unusual,' is his reply.

'I haven't been back here since I was a lad in the sixties. It hasn't changed that much. It's all coming back to me.'

'Goodness me,' he says. 'It's my patch. I've been coming at least twice a week for over 20 years. I live just around the corner, in Meols. Bird numbers are down over the years, and we get fewer rare birds too. I'm not sure if our numbers reflect the national decline or whether there's a local reason.'

We look around. The park is busy. Whilst we chat near a car park festooned with dimps, two cars arrive. Folk bringing their dogs.

'It's still good to come along,' he says, 'but the level of vandalism is getting serious, especially from those wankers from the Leasowe council estate. The sandhills have suffered badly.'

Unusually for me, I decide to hold my tongue.

Walking the sandhills rekindles another memory. All those years ago, a neighbour told me a story he had heard from his family of what went on in these very same dunes during the 19th century. Home to a notorious band of wreckers,[22] and one of them is supposed to haunt the lanes today. As boys we heard whispers from local farmers of a few notorious families involved in smuggling, mainly alcohol from Ireland.

There are several reports from the 19th century of wreckers lighting fires here on dark, stormy nights, to confound helmsmen making their way into Liverpool. Captains and navigators used landmarks to steer their way through shallow waters. We hear that false lights spread confusion and subsequent death. There is still debate as to whether the wreckers set out to wreck by deliberate act or whether they were simply the first on the salvage scene when ships ran aground.

The most famous wreck on these shores is chronicled in a Liverpool paper in 1838:

> Following the wreck here at Christmas 1838 of the packet ship Pennsylvania en route from Liverpool to New York during a hurricane-force storm we lament to find that these infamous wretches, the wreckers, have been at their fiendlike occupation, plundering what the elements have spared, instead of seeking to alleviate the calamities of their fellow creatures. The wreckers who infest the Cheshire coast were not long in rendering the catastrophe a source of emolument to themselves. The property of the passengers and crew were plundered by them to an alarming extent.

Another writer in 1863 noted,

> Wirral at that time […] was a desperate region, the inhabitants were nearly all wreckers and smugglers, they ostensibly carried on the trade and calling of fishermen, farm labourers and small farmers, but they were deeply saturated with the sin of covetousness, and many a fierce fire has been lighted on the Wirral shore on stormy nights to lure the good ship on the Burbo or Hoyle banks, there to beat and strain and throb until her timbers parted and her planks were floating in confusion on the stormy waves. Fine times then for the Cheshire men. On stormy days and nights, crowds might have been seen hurrying to the shore

---

22   For a delightful read about the local wreckers and smugglers along the north Wirral shoreline try *Wirral Smugglers, Wreckers and Pirates* by Gavin Chappell.

with carts, barrows, horses, asses, or oxen even which were made to draw timber, bales, boxes or anything that the raging waters might have cast up. Many a half-drowned sailor has had a knock on the sconce, whilst trying to obtain a footing that has sent him reeling back into the seething water, and many a house had been suddenly replenished with eatables and drinkables and furniture and garniture where previously bare walls and wretched accommodation only were visible.

There are many remote coastal areas around our shores replete with similar stories of smuggling and plunder. But what was it really like to scrape an agricultural living in these damp, low-lying pastures, liable to flood? Living conditions for agricultural workers were awful. So bad in fact, that most folk migrated to the mills of nearby Lancashire in search of a better life.

Were these Leasowe wreckers really 'saturated in the sin of covetousness', or is this another example of society's then attitude to the 'deserving poor', as exemplified in the new Victorian workhouses of the 1840s? A time of severe struggle. To use an unfortunate metaphor, there was a perfect storm of employment problems in the rural north-west at the time. Agricultural labouring wages were dreadful. There was no welfare other than the poor relief provided by the Church. The potato blight fungus which caused the Irish potato famine was also prevalent in Cheshire. The Great Hunger in Ireland caused significant immigration of starving Irish families into Cheshire and Lancashire. And as if all that was not enough, workers in the Lancashire mills were laid off as the Civil War in the American colonies reduced cotton imports to a trickle. In Wirral's coastal villages it was a desperate time.

Two carrion crows look down from their high perches on the white-washed lighthouse and take note of this senior visitor as the late-afternoon sun settles beneath the line of the raised embankment. Standing alone beneath the old Leasowe beacon, I am struck by the thought that my adult world makes more sense here. A settled contentment sits deep. As far as I can make out it's not nostalgia. I don't live here any more, but walking Leasowe's lanes, pastures and sandhills helps me get my bearings, helps me tackle those episodes when life throws up its challenges.

In adult life, do we unconsciously call on key judgements we made as adolescents to help us understand the world? When we navigate our way through some of the issues we face as adults, just how much of our decision making is already hard-wired in our minds by our formative experiences as youngsters? Just how much do our experiences in our teenage years form a grid of ideas and impressions against which we reflect our thoughts as adults? Just how much free will do we have?

Like me, this whitewashed lighthouse is past its prime. Are we both now just innocent bystanders? Did this old light look on impassively in those 150 years of service? Did it witness the shipwrecks? Was it numb and apathetic as Leasowe wreckers worked their malevolence? Did it see poverty and famine? Did it fashion a parental eye on us lads all those years ago?

Or have its memories, like its bricks, gone under the whitewash?

6

MELR AND THING-VOLLR

In 1938, when foundations were dug for a new car park of a Meols pub, The Railway, a wooden boat thought to be Viking in origin was found. The builders quickly covered it up, fearful of costly delays which might be incurred were it to be excavated. Thankfully one of them recorded a few measurements. It was 30 feet long and 5 feet wide, big enough to carry 20 to 30 Viking warriors and their goods. It is believed this boat was either a Viking transport boat, like a longship, or a ship from the centuries that immediately follow the Viking era. It had overlapping planks, typical of Viking clinker boats.

When the Vikings availed themselves of the deep-water basin at Meols (Melr) on the north Wirral coast, they were using a well-established port in this part of north-west England.

When the Viking settlement Dublin was sacked by a combined force of Irish clans in 902, many Norse families fled to England to avoid slaughter. They followed other Irish Vikings who had already come over to the Wirral for adventure. Some came seeking refuge from their tormentor, Harald Harfrági, son of Halfdan the Black, King of Vestfold; the new king had just unified Norway, and had scores to settle: blood feuds which went back to his father's day. The result of these migrations was a vibrant Viking community in the Wirral.

Wirral has the highest density of Old Norse place names in all of England. Indeed, in the 10th and 11th centuries it was a Norse settlement with its own boundary. Many villages here have names that end in the Viking by, meaning village or farm. Inland from Meols is damp marsh scrub, or *kjarr* in Norse. The place is now called Carr Fields and Carr Lane.

Wirral even had its own parliament, the *thing*, at Thingwall (Thing-Vollr), thought to be unique for the time. Archaeologists have determined the site of the legislative assembly to be the conical mound which so struck me when that ambulance, taking me as a ten-year old, drove down the sandstone lane to the sanatorium that saved my bacon.

The nearby settlement, close to Thingwall, established by these Irish Vikings was called in their day Íra-byr, which literally translates as 'Irish village or farm'. Today we know it as Irby.

The geography has not changed dramatically from those days of the Norsemen. I have sat on that seafront in Meols at Dove Point many times since my boyhood days, watching curlew and cormorant fly inland to the flat damp scrub, the carrs. The Railway pub, which probably has a Viking boat under its car park, is just a few hundred yards from where I sit looking out to sea, watching the horizon.

The soft breeze plays in my hair and, as I often do in times of reflection, I toy with my necklace. It's not a bling thing; it carries the simple message that I'm allergic to penicillin. A couple of ravens play in the damp meadows behind the embankment, their cronks soft in the gentle, sweet wind of late afternoon. I take off the bobble-hat; it's itching my scalp. My mind wanders, to the past with imagines some of those Norse settlers coming ashore, right here …

> Banks of oarsmen work hard as three longships crash
> through the surf. Oak keels grind on the hard grit of
> wet sand and ride up the pebble-strewn shore.
>
> A group of heathens, come to join their Norse brethren for a
> new life in Saxon England, haul their dragon boats beyond the
> high tide line. Beached. They are far from the protection and
> safety offered by the spirits of their homeland ancestors.
>
> Clad in coarse woollen cloaks tied by single metal clasps. Damp
> from the journey, their clothes cling to their hungry bodies.
>
> The three longships sit obliquely on their shallow, flat bottoms.
> Olaf, their leader, quickly has his crews inspect the boats.

*'Look,' gestures Olaf. 'These timbers need repair. We need to
seal these gaps. Make sure this is done in the next two days.' He
marks two split strakes now in need of the remedial fix. A mix
of tarred wool and animal hair to fill and seal any gaps.*

*'This sail is torn here,' he says. 'This will need
sewing.' The blood-red, heavy linen square sail from
his own vessel is ripped slightly in one corner.*

*A couple of men identify a suitable place to make camp. A
flat hollow in the dunes, only 100 fot [feet] from their boats.
Several men set to and construct a long single shelter. Three
heavy-duty linen awnings which cover the longships' decks
are used to build their own temporary longhouse.*

*A makeshift camp quickly takes shape. Ready within the hour.
Supplies needed for the next three days only are brought from the
longships. Driftwood, damp from the recently ebbed tide is collected,
but the fire is started with a few dry logs they have on board. The
fire's heat adds its own unique welcome to the makeshift bivouac.
Light and warmth spread under the canvas longhouse amidst the
dunes as several youngsters gather close to the fire, careful not to
get in the way of their mothers preparing the cooking area.*

*Two women slow-roast skewered mackerel caught
during the voyage. A large cauldron is suspended over
the fire from a portable pyramidal iron frame.*

*As the newly arrived long-hairs sit to eat, dipping
their wooden spoons into the communal cauldron,
there is the hard, rhythmic sound of wings.*

'Ravens.'

They look up into the dim light.

*Ominous. The crews know that ravens are the eyes and ears of their
supreme god of war, Odin.[23] What does it mean? They watch in*

---

23 Whenever Odin appears in sagas, he carries a couple of ravens who travel the world for
him and bring back useful information. Ravens collect in the skies over the dead bodies
after battle, waiting for the armies to move on. In this way they foretell death. They are
omens. To Vikings, it is no coincidence that their plumage is all black. We still have our
own omen-ravens, alive and well in the Tower of London.

silence and wonder as the flock of eleven pass directly overhead, their occasional deep guttural cronks carry then fade in the wind. The flock continues in a straight line out to sea. Soon just dots and then gone …

Olaf is over 6 feet, a commanding figure, still in his mid-twenties. He takes off his rough, salt-stained leather skullcap. His knotted fair hair fills out in the breeze and falls onto his broad shoulders. He strokes his beard and full moustache, twirling the facial hairs around his dark fingers. His battle-scarred face and hands add authority. He deftly coils his straying locks into a bun and puts his headgear back on, making sure the decorative raven image in black stitching sits across his forehead.

'The signs are good,' declares Olaf. 'The ravens have given us their blessing.'

Around Olaf's neck is a piece of flat, thin, pale whalebone, no bigger than the size of his buckle, hung on a heavy thread. It carries the plain inscription of an arrowhead, pointing upwards. At this moment in their lives, they need all the good fortune they can muster and this runic symbol says it all. Victory. Olaf carefully and deliberately strokes the rune as he speaks, knowing these runes carry magical powers. His men are impressed.

'The voyage over from Dublin went well. We have a new life here in the Wirral.' Olaf uses the Old English name. 'Now is the time to get some sleep after the journey. We have had a long day; we're exhausted but glad to be here. Safe.'

The sound of a piping oystercatcher breaks my reverie. The wind continues to play in my own hair, the ravens playing in the meadow have flown, and a few drops of rain fall on the embankment where I sit. The dream of Olaf fades but the smell of their cooking lingers in my nostrils.

As a young lad, home after a day's birding, Ma often had a pot of 'scouse' waiting on the stove. It couldn't have been that different from what was in the cauldron I'd imagined on the beach. Indeed, the term was introduced to Merseyside by our Viking settlers, only they spelt it 'skause'.[24]

---

24 Traditional 'skause' – a mix of fresh vegetables and cheap cuts of mutton boiled up together, along with anything else that was on the go. Excellent with a thick slice of bread, door-stopper style.

As a middle-aged man, my hands began to suffer from tight tendons, especially in the left hand, affecting my grip. I just happened to mention the condition to Tony, my GP. I must have been there for something else as the condition was not serious, just a nuisance.

'Agh, you have the early beginnings of Viking disease,' he said. He told me the condition is called Dupuytren's contracture. He explained it's a condition in which one or more fingers become permanently bent in a flexed position due to abnormal thickening of tissue just beneath the skin. This thickening occurs in the palm and can extend into the fingers. Hard thick lines of bumps and cords develop which can cause the fingers to bend into the palm.

'Why is it called the Viking disease?' I asked Tony. 'Was it all that rowing?'

'Very funny,' he replied, without even a hint of a smile. 'It's a condition prevalent in Norway, where 30 per cent of men over 65 have the condition. Elsewhere in the world only 5–10 per cent of the male population have it. In Asian and Black communities it's unheard of.'

7

HILBRE

Birding trips, especially to Hilbre, are organised by consulting tide tables in the *Liverpool Echo* or those in the library. The state of the tide dictates where we go and what we might see. Roy tells us that tides result from the closeness of the moon. How can this be? We consult the local library again and soak up and share knowledge. Apparently it's all down to gravity. Well not quite all.

We know that tides result from the effects of both gravity and inertia. Some would say a clash between these two forces of nature, but nature always finds an equilibrium, if there is one to be found. The tide, rushing in at walking pace over the sandbank towards our embankment, is in effect the result of a balance between the pull of the moon and the inertia of the huge body of water. The earth rotates once every 23 hours, 56 minutes and 4.09053 seconds, the sidereal period. The earth's circumference is roughly 40,075 kilometres. Thus any point on the equator moves at a speed of 460 metres per second, which is roughly 1,000 miles per hour.

The moon's gravitational pull is quite small compared to earth's. The tides are more to do with the earth's spinning on its axis, where a centrifugal force combined with gravity causes our tide. As the earth rotates, the moon completes one orbit in our sky approximately every 25 hours. In most places on the planet we get two tidal peaks as well as two tidal troughs in this 25-hour cycle; a new high tide normally arrives every 12 hours and 25.25 minutes, to be precise.

More difficult to fathom are the different heights of our tides. We see high tides threaten the dunes and we may naturally think autumnal gales must be associated with these exceptional tides – but no. An early science lesson: do not rely exclusively on what seems to be common sense. The name 'spring' derives from these exceptional tides springing forth twice each lunar month. They have nothing to do with the season of the year, but occur when the sun and moon are aligned with our earth. Spring tides at Leasowe are approximately 20 per cent higher than its normal tides. Neap tides on the other hand occur when the sun and moon's gravitational pull do not combine but, pulling at right angles to one another, cancel each other out to some degree. Consequently, neap tides have the lowest difference in depth between high and low tides. Neap tides also occur twice every lunar month.

Getting to Hilbre is not going to be easy. A leisurely walk across from West Kirby takes an hour, slightly less if in a hurry, and once the tide surrounds the islands it's another four hours before we can leave. Our trip must happen on a weekend or during the school holidays, and we need a day when high tide is at noon or just before.

Tide tables are checked. We agree a date and time: West Kirby at six in the morning, which means leaving home on my bike at five.

The slow journey on my Raleigh in the dimly lit hours of early morning against the prevailing westerly is interrupted by an observant bobby. What's a young lad doing, cycling along at five-thirty on a dark Sunday morning with a canvas rucksack in the middle of all these grand houses of Hoylake?

'Tell me, young man,' he asks. 'How old are you?'

'Thirteen,' I reply.

'Where have you come from, and where are you going?' His thin chinstrap sits loosely on his square jaw.

'I've cycled from Leasowe and I'm going to West Kirby,' I reply, nearly calling him Mr Dixon (of Dock Green).

The word 'Leasowe' is enough to make him suspicious. 'Okay, let's have a look in your bag. And precisely what are you doing at this unearthly hour, may I ask?' he says, with just a hint of a smug grin.

'I'm going bird-watching to Hilbre and it's all my gear for the day,' I reply, delivering it in a slightly cocky way.

A roll of his eyes: '*Really*? Let me have a look, then.'

A quick peek into the Army & Navy olive-green canvas bag reveals a thermos flask, sarnies, an apple and biscuits as well as binoculars and a notebook. His not unreasonable curiosity is sated, followed swiftly by a look of disappointed bemusement if not mild disdain. 'On your way, then,' he says. He could easily have muttered, 'It takes all sorts.'

It's first light on a cold May morning when I meet up with Mac and Roy. We park our bikes, locked to the railings in West Kirby, near the slipway to the sands. A solitary blackbird offers its gentle melodic song, a reminder of full light to come. The creeping crescendo of a dawn chorus erupts as we step out, due west, across the sands to Little Eye. Beyond, the lights of North Wales flicker.

The immediate sands near to the embankment are soft and generous, untouched by the tide's impact. Day trippers will come here later in the summer for their donkey rides and candyfloss. A few yards further out, beyond the strand line, harder sands beckon, patterned with repeat ripples made by the tide's oscillating waves. Lugworm leftovers cover the stretch. Coiled castings of discarded nutrient-free sand.

Looking back to where we left our bikes, the soft orange light of the rising sun brightens the sky behind the silhouettes of West Kirby's grander residences. Homes to some of Liverpool's mercantile class.

The westerly is blowing hard directly into our faces; heads are down as we trudge on in our wellies. Here the Dee Estuary is littered with cockle beds. Discarded razor clam shells lie strewn on damp sand. An oystercatcher raises the alarm; its rifling, piping sound echoes across deserted mudflats. Walking out into darkness, we see ahead of us some streetlights glimmering in the far distance – but that is North Wales, a good 3 or 4 miles away. The tide is on the turn. For this young lad there is safety in numbers as we trudge out into the gloom, reassured that it will soon be daylight.

Little Eye is half a mile out. The first of three islands to be freed by the night's retreating tide. Little Eye is lit by the ascending low sun to our backs, and in the distance the brooding mountains of North Wales show in faint outline.

Yet another world to explore one day in our young, never-ending, futures.

A quick recce of this tiny island throws up a few carrion crows but little else. A right turn to north, to Middle Eye, carefully avoids the slippy, seaweed-drenched sandstone outcrops.

Waders occupy a few rock pools: probing redshank, a single curlew, yet more oystercatchers and a few turnstones. Crows scavenge for scraps, think nothing of tackling a mussel, using their massive beaks to lever open the bivalve. Herring gulls have another technique, flying up to 20 feet to drop the shell on hard rock below, knowing that after several attempts it will eventually crack open.

A narrow, short path at Middle Eye's southern point climbs the sandstone to a flat, grassy surface, an area equivalent to a long, thin football pitch covering the hard sandstone. A perimeter of smooth, curved, red wave-worn cliffs surrounds a plateau of wind-blown bramble thickets and newly uncurled fern. A wheatear, resting during its northerly migration, checks out the sandstone's nooks for invertebrates. Once the sun is up, barn swallows will catch flying insects here. There is no easy path to walk Middle Hilbre's perimeter. Finds include a few meadow pipits and a single dunnock. Crows comb the shoreline. Gulls lurk for trade.

As I look back to West Kirby, the morning's soft light shimmers delicately on the incoming tide. A tide which knows where to flow, where to meander, where to fill those shallow pools. Diminutive waders, probably sanderling, follow the water's incoming edge. A closer inspection identifies a few ringed plover. Hilbre is just 100 yards from Middle Hilbre. All three islands sit on flat sedimentary beds, ancient contorted upliftings. Deposited many millions of years ago. Thin layers, like hard-set icing sugar on a freshly baked cake. Layered, sandstone-tide ripples. (*Photos 20, 21 and 22*)

A depression in the surface layer runs between Middle Hilbre and Hilbre. A pathway. A fault line 6 feet wide and a foot deep. Waxy underfoot. Greasy. Flat ribbons of brown seaweed fronds litter the surface. A path which follows the rock's natural contours reaches a stretch of shingle and sand. From here it's much easier: a gravel pathway, big enough for a vehicle, climbs the shallow rise to Hilbre, the largest of the three islands, 11.5 acres of green grass and red sandstone, less than half a mile long.

Ahead, set back from the path, are several old houses close to the east cliffs. The first cottage, to the right, belongs to the warden; adjacent to the cottage is a wooden frame of wire mesh, covering 70 square yards or so of shrubs.

'There's the Heligoland trap,' says Mac. 'I think it's the only one in the north-west.'

'He is keen,' I think.

This trap has the footprint of a large cottage. A frame of stout timbers supports a covering of chicken-wire, like a transparent shroud, over an area of bushes and shrubs where birds naturally congregate and feed. Open at one end, the trap tapers to a narrow funnel, and at the right moment the birds are chased down the funnel into a small cage. The entrance lid to the cage is dropped and the birds are then carefully removed and fitted with a small leg ring.[25] A glimpse into the adult world of serious ornithology.

Just like Middle Hilbre, the main island's exposed red sandstone has been eroded by wind and tide to form a perimeter of rounded, worn cliffs, 20 to 30 feet above seaweed-covered boulders below. The emerald-green grass turf on the island carries a variety of plants. Small, coral-white flowers of sea thrift, and clusters of delicate sea pink. Rare rock sea-lavender, a small herb with violet-blue flowers, protrudes from one or two rock crevices.

At the northern end, near the old boathouse, the sea swells in a deep inlet where a seal, a young female, surfaces to peer at us. An Atlantic grey seal, to use her proper name. She turns and swims back out to sea, probably to rejoin her colony over towards North Wales.

An adult sandwich tern passes overhead. Its sharp and rasping 'kreik, kreik' fills the air. It's the size of a small gull but with long, elegant, tapered white wings. Adult male and female sandwich terns have almost identical plumages so I have no idea of its gender, but my mind, drawing on knowledge below the conscious level, says female. She turns her head to me and

---

25 A light aluminium ring is attached to one leg by a licensed ringer. On the ring is a unique reference number with a request to inform the British Trust for Ornithology (BTO) if found. The ringer records the species, gender, date, weight and a few key measurements. Other details such as probable age may also be kept. These details are then transferred to a central register kept by the BTO. Records are later referenced whenever the BTO is con- tacted, often when a corpse is found with a ring, or when the bird is re-trapped. This cen- tral registry offers a rich source of migration information which initially offered insights into migration routes. However, they have been recording bird numbers and patterns for over 60 years(https://www.bto.org/our-science)

glares for a few seconds before returning her gaze to the sea below. She's on the lookout and suddenly closes her wings and dives into the water, collecting a tiny silvery fish in her nearly all-black beak. If you look carefully, there's a yellow tip. She moves on, past the boathouse and out to sea. Gone.

A male northern wheatear pops up on a wall near the telegraph station, his plumage quite distinct from that of the female. He's a summer visitor, the size of a large robin, and has recently arrived from Africa. Settled on a smooth sandstone outcrop, alert to the world and to me. He's so close I can see my own miniature reflection in his dark shiny eye. He's exhausted – probably arrived overnight. His distinct features of a slate-grey back and black ear coverts are striking. His chest is white with gentle, soft, rufous hints of orange. Suddenly he's had enough and flies off behind the telegraph station. A stunning bird. Will he nest on the island, or is he just stopping for a few hours to feed before moving on further north? There's no sign of a mate. Where is he bound? Ireland, northern England, Scotland, maybe the Shetlands?

'Has recently arrived from Africa.' Five little words which pack so much. One day, after five months in the sub-tropics, he decides to move north. He crosses the Sahara, then the Mediterranean, then France or Spain before navigating the Channel and coming up our west coast. Another 'why?' in our black notebooks. Like millions of birds, his migration is a feat of endurance and navigation. He travels alone.

Where the gravel path descends to the sea at the south of Hilbre, a small green-yellowish bird darts behind loose sandstone rock fragments from a recent cliff-fall. A warbler perhaps? Time to sit down and wait. It will be another three hours before the tide ebbs and we can leave. Ten minutes later a willow warbler emerges, feeding on the ground, looking for small insects and spiders. Its sharp creamy-white supercilium softens in the dappled light. The bird's olive-green upperparts and yellowy-white underparts match the background of grass and sand. A smashing little find. My presence is obviously no threat. A joy to watch. No time pressures. After 20 minutes the warbler flies around the low cliff corner, to the tiny, quaintly named Niffy Bay.

A hundred yards across the water, a mixed group of oystercatchers, redshank, curlew and dunlin roost on a minute shingle shore on Middle Hilbre. They will be there, unmolested, until the tide recedes.

The boathouse at the northern point of Hilbre is our own high-tide roost. Huge rectanguloid sandstone blocks form a wide slipway which descends as far as the sea, even at low tide. Severe storms have cast a few of these massive slabs, like playthings, along the island's nearby eastern shore. The roof of the boathouse has long since gone, if it ever had one. The sea here carries a fine silt suspension; a light, yellowy-brown tinge.

When strong winds in the Irish Sea push migrating seabirds towards the coast's natural shelter, there is no better place to be than Hilbre's boathouse, to marvel at the passing avian caravan. Glimpses of birds of the open seas: scoters, divers, skuas, terns, auks, gannets, shearwaters.

Three older birders, in their early twenties, join us on the slipway. One of them, the tallest, asks, 'Anything about?'

'A female wheatear and a willow warbler,' says Mac.

'Yes, we saw the wheatear. Where's the willie?'

Mac tells them exactly where, and they make a few notes.

'What about out to sea?' asks the tallest.

'Our count today includes three common scoter, eight gannets, four razorbills and twenty-one guillemots.'

'Not bad. Your first time here?' the same guy asks.

'Yes, we came on our bikes from Leasowe and Wallasey,' I reply.

We are deferential, delighted they are including us in their conversations. They ask us a few questions: where we go to school and how long we've been birdwatching. We gather they are all from Liverpool University and come over whenever they can. I ask one of them to tell us about Hilbre.

They are happy to oblige. One of the group – I miss his name – says, 'My subject's geology, so let's start there. The red and yellow sandstone all around us was laid down in the Triassic era. That's over 200 million years ago.'

I'm pleased he tells us, even though I have no idea what 'Triassic' means. He goes on to say that footprints of a prehistoric animal, either a bear or an ape, have been found in the sandstone. He is not sure where exactly.

Another guy, the one with a blue bobble hat, pipes up: 'The name "Hilbre" is thought to come from Saint Hildeburgh, an Anglo-Saxon woman who was living on the island in the 7th century as a religious recluse.'[26]

The same guy continues: 'Hilbre's been inhabited continuously since the Stone Age. That's over 5,000 years. Some bits and pieces from that period were found in 1926. We think it was once a hermitage, and we know for sure that Benedictine monks established a cell and a small church here in 1080.'

'Wow,' says Roy, as he looks around. 'Some history.'

It's fascinating stuff, and terrific to have these guys explain it all on our first visit. The tall guy – I think his name is Dave – explains that he teaches zoology.

'In the late Jurassic period the first bird appears in fossil records. Not from Hilbre, you understand,' he quickly adds. 'Archaeopteryx evolved directly from reptiles. As their wings were originally forelimbs, the bill evolved to do lots of things which once were the work of those forelimbs – their hands and arms.'

'Wow,' I think, 'this is all news to me.' I want to find out more. 'I'm sorry,' I say, 'but what do you mean when you say birds evolved from reptiles. How does that work?'

'Well, in a nutshell,' says possible Dave, 'over millions of years, some species of lizards have slowly changed through mutation, and the changes which work for them mean they survive. Any mutations that hinder their survival mean they die off. It's not a sudden change but a series of small changes over millions of years.' He leaves it at that. I don't understand, but don't have the courage to ask yet again. We listen intently, deferentially.

'Evolution works in many ways. Let's take one feature, a bird's beak. Did you spot any dunlins on your way over?' says possible Dave.

Mac replies, 'Yes; there were a few in the rock pools between Middle Hilbre and Hilbre.'

'Well, these little fellers, as well as other birds which search for food in the sand, like knot and godwits, have evolved a feature on their top

---

26 With such a religious heritage it is easy to see why Hilbre became a centre for pilgrimage in the 13th and 14th centuries. At the dissolution of the monasteries (1536–1541) two monks remained on the island for a very practical reason – they maintained an important beacon for shipping in the river mouth – but this arrangement didn't last long: the last monk left the island around 1550 as it was no longer considered a sanctuary, having become a centre for commerce and a busy trading port. A custom house was established to collect taxes on goods traded up and down the River Dee.

mandible which they can bend. It's a bit like your fingertip. They use it to detect lugworms in the mud. Many wading birds have this feature, called distal rhynchokinesis. It's a big word made up of three little ones: ryncho is an upper mandible, kinesis means movement, and distal means 'far from the point of attachment', in this case the end of the bill. It's a long name for what is simply a flexible end to the top mandible.' (*Photo 23*)

Possible Dave looks at us to see if we have taken that on board.

It's Roy who has the confidence to respond. 'Very interesting,' he says. 'Is that something unique to birds that feed in the mud?'

'I guess so,' says possible Dave. 'These birds can't see their prey; they have to feel for lugworms or whatever in the mud. They also have a little sensor on the tip of their bill that can detect the movement of anything living down there.'

'What about oystercatchers?' says Roy.

'I'm not sure, but I don't think so. Their bills are stout and strong. They use this strength to break open muscles and cockles,' says possible Dave. 'Did you see any curlews?

'Sure,' says Roy.

'Curlews prefer wet sand. Their bills are slender and they can penetrate deeper, but the sand or mud needs to be soft. You'll often see them in the channels as the tide goes out. Ideal territory for them.'

This is getting to be a one-to-one conversation, with the rest of us listening intently. Mac, wanting to join in, changes the subject. 'Do you catch much in the Heligoland trap? Do you guys ring them?'

'Aye we do,' says the guy in a blue bobble-hat. 'We're running a bird observatory. We normally check the trap in the morning. Some migrating birds may have decided to make Hilbre a place to recover after a long flight. We often get many migrants after a shitty night, when it's been overcast and raining.'

My confidence is coming back, and I ask, 'Are there any other bird observatories like Hilbre?'

'Yes, quite a few. The nearest is on Bardsey Island, off the Llyn Peninsula, North Wales, then there's Portland Bill in Dorset, Dungeness in Kent, the Isle of May in the Firth of Forth in Scotland, and Spurn Point at the mouth of the Humber. We shouldn't forget Fair Isle, the remote island between the Orkneys and the Shetlands.'

'It's a network,' says blue bobble-hat. 'If you want to visit any of them let us know and we'll give you the details.' But his look suggested we were a bit young still.

'Do they all have Heligoland traps, like yours?' asks Mac.

'Yep, and most have mist nets as well.'

The tall one, possible Dave, takes a quick look at his watch. 'Sorry, lads, but it's time we had a brew.' He picks up his rucksack and makes for the hole in the wall, where once was a possible door. The two others follow.

'See yer,' we all say, as if we are now good friends and we had met them many times before. We sit down against the boathouse wall, open our food boxes and pour our drinks.

'What's a mist net?' says I.

'I think it's a fine-mesh net which traps birds safely. It's portable and so you can choose where to use it,' says Mac.

He talks of how he might join a ringing group … but I'm still wondering: just how did those reptiles change into birds?

The sea is calmer now; the bite in the wind has gone. More of the slipway shows, and Roy, who has a watch too, suggests it will soon be time to leave. We make our way to the south end, and sure enough the tide has receded enough for us to walk over to Middle Hilbre, careful not to slip on green algae-covered, flat, wet sandstone slabs. Clumps of bladderwrack, their pale green fronds covered in blister-like air bubbles, dry out on adjacent rockpools.

We make Middle Hilbre and cross over the island via the one narrow path. A fine male kestrel sits on a fence post and looks at us through those narrow, dark, round eyes.

'Do you think if we don't look at him directly, he might not fly away?' Mac suggests.

We pass by calmly and slowly without looking his way, and sure enough he lingers. One more to Mac.

We start out across the sands for West Kirby. Little terns with their yellow beaks, accompanied by bigger sandwich terns, fish the same channel as the tide ebbs. It seems terns prefer to fish on retreating tides.

Resting for a moment, we turn around and take in the view. A redshank is caught, backlit in the setting sun's focused bright light. (*Photo 24*)

The North Wales backdrop offers another world, now silhouetted and indistinct. The low sun sets behind those far hills. It's dusk. Light fades. A silver sheen lies over wet sandbanks, reflecting what little miserly light there is. We tramp the final yards in silence, back to West Kirby, 11 hours since we locked up our bikes. I look over my shoulder for a final *coup d'oeil* at Hilbre before setting off for the bike ride home in the dark.

We don't need to tell each other; we know birding will never be the same for us.

Did we leave behind our playful boyhood shenanigans on the 11-acre grassy isle? Ask the question, scratch the surface, peel the onion. Was it at Hilbre that my serious quest for more knowledge began? To be on this search, to try and understand and fathom out nature's intricacies only works to reinforce the wonder and awe of it all. It's going to be a magnificent journey of discovery.

As we ride off on our bikes, 'I fancy Bardsey Island,' says Mac.

'I'm up for it,' I quickly add.

'Me too,' says Roy.

'Next summer?'

Fifty years later, I trace Mac down to his place in Norfolk. Our chat is largely of those days at Hilbre.

'Hilbre was the gamechanger for me,' he says. 'I was hooked from that first visit when we all met at West Kirby on our bikes. I went back again as often as I could. I got to know the warden and would leave my bike in his front garden at West Kirby. I remember I was late one day. He left me a note saying he would meet me on Hilbre. But when I got to Middle Hilbre the crossing to Hilbre was already under water, so I waded out holding my rucksack over my head. A wave knocked me over, but I managed to get back on my feet and make it to the shingle shore. I didn't mind, and I thought he'd be pleased – but he gave me one almighty bollocking.'

'How old were you then?' I ask.

'Fifteen, I think,' he replies. Mac was always the one to take risks.

'Hilbre meant a lot to me too,' I tell Mac.

'How's that?' he asks.

'Well, it's a long time ago, but I do remember feeling stupid that I didn't understand what one of those university guys meant by evolution. Do you remember on our first visit, one of them told us that birds evolved from reptiles?'

'Sorry,' says Mac, 'I don't remember.'

'I've been fascinated with evolution ever since.'

8

SNOWDROP

A warm, early October morning and low sun sits at my young straight back whilst I gaze out on the vast expanse of the Irish Sea. Exploration has taken us westward, towards Moreton, Meols, Hoylake, West Kirby and Hilbre Island. Today I'm taking the opposite direction, along the embankment that runs eastwards to Wallasey Village, where I will meet Mac and Roy, and then we will head off to New Brighton and the River Mersey.

Just a few hundred yards from the sand dunes, the embankment path meets a wide road, shielded from the sea's swell by a shoulder-high wall.[27]

Several fishermen patiently wait for the next low tide, to harvest the cod and whiting they hope will have taken the baits on the 50-metre lines they have fixed to the seabed. A few concrete ramps, left exposed by the tide, hold bands of foraging turnstones, the first waders to explore what the ebbing tide has to offer.

This new stretch of the coast is close and compact, in contrast to the wide-open sands of Mockbeggar Wharf and Hoyle Bank. The sea is immediate and tight to these impregnable vertical granite walls. Even in today's calm conditions, seas surge and flow, swirl and froth, heavy with intent. Black-headed gulls, hang stationary, facing into the onshore wind, looking for floating scraps.

---

27 The King's Parade Sea Wall was constructed in the 1930s, over 12 feet tall and covering just under 1.5 miles of coastline, to protect the hinterland from flooding. The wall was built with a curved front designed to reduce the impact of the waves and increase the wall's lifespan. The destructive energy in these at times violent waves is thus reflected back out to sea, and the rate at which the wall is worn away is reduced considerably.

This granite wall runs all the way from Wallasey Village to New Brighton, where a man-made marine lake needs inspecting. A few forsaken sailing dinghies, soon to be lifted out of the water and taken to their covered winter quarters, are moored to a pontoon. Their halliards smack a complicated tinny rhythm on metal masts.

The lake holds common shore crabs and is frequented by visiting diving sea ducks. We are in luck: two cormorants, not exactly ducks, are working the lake. They sit low in the buoyant salt water, their thin necks giving them a snake-like, reptilian look. The nearest cormorant surfaces with tangled weed, and its further dives prove equally futile. At high tide the marine lake attracts waders from the feeding ground of the Mersey estuary's sand banks. Hundreds of redshank, dunlin and turnstone jostle for limited space. A close scan reveals two purple sandpipers.

A strange name to give these characterful waders, as in their breeding plumage, when waders are at their most colourful, there is no purple at all. Their upperparts are dark grey, but in winter their feathers carry a pale lavender tinge. Short, yellow legs give them a squat, plump appearance. Underparts are white.

Purple sandpipers feed on molluscs, other marine invertebrates and occasional plant material, but unlike many waders they do not feed by blind probing of their beaks into sand or soil, preferring to pick up food on the surface by sight.

It is likely that the birds we see on the west coast during winter, like these two, have flown in from eastern Canada and Newfoundland in one non-stop flight; an amazing feat for such a little bird, but then they have a lot of daring.

Of all the waders feeding on the rocky shoreline during an incoming tide, the stout purple sandpipers are the last to abandon a favourite feeding spot, clinging to wave-splashed, seaweed-covered boulders. At the very last second, to avoid an incoming wave, up they go, just a few feet, and descend to the same spot once the rock is free again. Daredevil behaviour and fascinating to watch. (*Photo 25*)

In the distance we see Liverpool's waterfront. Not for the first time this view evokes images of young John, Paul, George and Pete – or should that be Ringo? – and their raw energy in song. Our city is on the map as never before. We are not quite scousers; we are woolly-backs, from across the water. I prefer to think of this part of the Wirral as Liverpool's left bank.

We make for the confluence of the Mersey and Liverpool Bay. The river here is at its narrowest; Liverpool is tantalisingly close. (*Photo 26*) As the tide begins to ebb, wave-worn lines of dark-brown sandstone covered in a green moss-like seaweed begin to show near New Brighton's Perch Rock lighthouse. Strong tidal currents carry drifting black-headed gulls out to the bay, only for them to fly back upstream to repeat their drift with the churned-up waters of the retiring tide. Rockpools reveal several ringed plover. A sandwich tern fishes, hanging 10 feet above the pools. Oystercatchers are quick to return to the newly exposed sandbanks and start feeding afresh. Herring gulls return to their favourite seaweed-strewn, almost black, sandstone, with roosting in mind.

A ferry approaches the nearby New Brighton pier, and in the distance one of Canadian Pacific's passenger boats, probably *Empress of Canada*, is tied up at the pier head. She tracks across the North Atlantic between Liverpool and Montreal; confirmation, if it was ever in doubt, that cosmopolitan Liverpool faces westward to Ireland and the New World. A massive yellow and lime-green liner with a single, slanting funnel, hints at glamorous cruises.

The nearby ferry, *Royal Daffodil*, is now alongside the pier at New Brighton. Ropes are thrown to the guys at the pier's capstans, seas churn as engaged propellers fight the tide. Once the vessel is secured, ramps are lowered from the pontoon onto its passenger decks, allowing passengers to disembark before gates open to let new passengers board the ferry back across the Mersey.

Across the river at this pinch point, docks stretch northwards from the pier head along the Liverpool shoreline to Bootle and beyond. A river busy with traffic. The wind blows black smoke plumes from many funnels, like dark, horizontal pennants. Tugboats nudge hulls or pull on taut ropes. Ferries weave their crossings in this busy river against the backdrop of Liverpool's three graces: the Royal Liver Building, the Cunard Building and the Port of Liverpool Building, the centrepieces of Liverpool's waterfront heritage. The overhead dock railway known locally as the docker's umbrella, runs the length of the waterfront, looking like a scene from *The French Connection*. The city sprawls eastwards behind this busy river. Away from the waterfront she boasts splendid Georgian architecture: Stanley Park, St George's Hall and Lime Street station, not forgetting Penny Lane and Strawberry Fields.

Fast forward 50 years. Birdwatching from Perch Rock in New Brighton has not changed. It is still a great place to be when September storms batter the coast.

The original perch, first erected in 1683, was a triangular tripod of timber which carried a lantern to warn shipping of submerged rocks. By the 19th century a more robust lighthouse was needed, and its construction, started in 1827, of Anglesey granite coincided with the erection, on the same rocky outcrop, of a fort to guard the entrance to the Mersey.[28]

Traffic to the old docks and dockers' livelihoods dried up as soon as the container port at Seaforth opened in 1971, just 4 miles upstream from the pier head. Today, an odd cargo boat and an occasional oil tanker head for the refinery at upstream Stanlow, near Ellesmere Port. The Empress boats to Canada are gone, their customers having long since succumbed to the dubious delights of flying.

Daily ferries now connect Liverpool and Birkenhead to Dublin, Isle of Man and Belfast – but that's it. The docks lie derelict or, in the case of Albert Dock, are converted into shops, museums, restaurants and a northern home for the Tate. The bustling Liverpool Marina has taken over the old Coburg Wharf.

All that is left of the ferries across the Mersey of my youth is a river cruise aboard *Snowdrop* and a few crossings by *Royal Iris*. The original Wallasey ferries were named after places on the Wirral including Seacombe, Egremont, Mountwood, Woodchurch (a huge Birkenhead overspill council estate, known locally as Dodge City) and yes, good old

28   The good merchants of Liverpool had first mooted the idea of a fort guarding the entrance to Mersey back in Napoleonic times, but it was not completed until 1829, using local red sandstone. It housed over 100 men and had a battery of 18 guns. Ships bound for Liverpool and Birkenhead had to use the only navigable part of the river, here known as the Rock Channel, which was only 900 yards away. The fort's guns were used only twice before it was decommissioned in 1956.

Leasowe. These ferries connected the towns of Wallasey and Birkenhead to the bustle, trade and international travel centre which was Liverpool.

Tourists wanting to see the Mersey by boat take a short river cruise on *Snowdrop*, the latest reincarnation of the old ferry, MV *Woodchurch*. It is colourfully dressed in the dazzle style of camouflage, much used in the First World War to make life difficult for U-boat commanders trying to judge their target's range, speed and heading. The name 'Snowdrop' harks back to the time when these quintessential ferries used names of flowers. The landing stages are still in good repair, but gone is the ferry terminal at New Brighton. A Beatles 'Day Tripper' to New Brighton now arrives by rail, and the old green and yellow-liveried *Royal Iris*, the exemplar of its day, sits rotting in a Liverpool dock.

When I was a boy, everyone had family associations with the maritime world which sprung out of Liverpool and Birkenhead: casual labour in the docks, office work in the port's trading companies and shipping lines, and much sought-after apprenticeships at Cammell Lairds, the shipbuilders. Merchant seamen brought home not just tales of their travels but also vinyl 78s from New York, Chicago and New Orleans. Liverpool still looks overseas for its wealth, and particularly towards old Empire. A strong Irish connection and a thriving Chinese community adds to its uniqueness. It's an open city and, in many ways, so not English.

Liverpool does have a difficult past, kept under wraps until the 1980s, when fresh light was shed on its role in the slave trade.

Whereas in the days of my youth there had been no public mention whatsoever of the slave trade, the first civic reference to it was in 1980, when the Merseyside Maritime Museum opened and showed a few exhibits. There then followed a dedicated Transatlantic Slavery Gallery in 1994; and finally, in 2007, the International Slavery Museum was opened, 200 years after the Slave Trade Act of 1807 had officially abolished the trade in slaves in the British Empire – but not, it should be noted, slavery itself. (The Act had encouraged Britain to press for the abolition of the trade in slaves in other countries – but it was not until 1833, when the Slavery Abolition Act was passed, that slavery itself was abolished in all parts of the British Empire.)

Merchants and master mariners financed this triangular win–win trade by bringing in cotton from American colonies, unloading their cargo in Liverpool's growing number of new wet docks and then selling the cheap unprocessed cotton to the mill owners of Manchester and Lancashire, who had rapidly become wealthy. The new docks meant quicker turnaround times, as it was possible to unload at low tide as well as high. Once emptied of their raw cotton, the vessels would be loaded with manufactured goods and ammunition. These goods were traded along the coasts of west Africa for slaves, who were then transported to the Caribbean and the southern states of America. Many slaves died on this cramped and perilous journey, but those who did make it were sold, and the boats were then loaded with raw cotton bound for Liverpool. A toxic, tragic triangle.

Three quarters of all European slave ships left from Liverpool. The Liverpool traders alone shipped a total of one and half million black Africans, in horrendous conditions, across the Atlantic to the Caribbean and southern states of America.

Personal fortunes were made during the 200 years of this trade. The physical infrastructure required to support this trade is still visible, of course, in the city. Grandiose buildings which housed cotton exchanges, all the major banks, finance houses, customs buildings and port authorities, grace the city. The trading infrastructure of the canals used to take goods to and from Liverpool's massive ribbon of docks remain, but gone is the central overhead railway running along the entire length of the docks. Demolished in 1957.

Liverpool's sordid past is a story worth repeating over and over; easily overlooked, conveniently forgotten. The wealth to build many of the great houses which surround Liverpool Bay in areas like Bidston, Oxton, West Kirby, Hoylake, Meols, Crosby, Formby, St Annes and Southport came directly from the slave trade. The affluent magnates of 'Cottonopolis' (Manchester) and other Lancashire towns amassed their fortunes from the processing of the cheap raw cotton. Fortunes which were spent on building palaces on the Wirral, the Fylde Coast and even as far afield as the Lake District and Anglesey – all locations which lie to the north or west of the factories of Manchester and Lancashire. The prevailing westerlies took the industrial air pollution eastwards, into the Pennine villages.

There is one tale in my family which touches tangentially on Liverpool's heady times of shipping and commerce.

I am in my late forties when I find myself in Buenos Aires, negotiating a deal to secure an agency agreement to import into the UK wines from a top family estate in Argentina's premium wine region, Mendoza, high in the Andean foothills. I have successfully negotiated with the son who manages all commercial matters for this international business. The other son is the winemaker. We agree volumes, prices, credit and so on – but there is one final hurdle to overcome: their dad needs to finally approve the deal. We are invited to dinner at their ranch in the outskirts of Buenos Aires. The two sons are fluent in English, but he is not. I should add that in my short list of talents, foreign language skills don't figure.

Father employs his own translator, who sits on his right. His charming wife is on his left. We all sit at a round table with the two sons and their wives. My place is directly opposite the father, across the full diameter of the circle. He's a traditional guy. Extremely polite, a generous man, immensely proud of his two boys, and meticulously dressed. He's a key figure in the Argentine wine renaissance. One of his legacies is his passion for obscure grape varieties. He has a nursery of several old species of vine which he has collected. A man with a deep sense of place and purpose. A man to be respected.

We enjoy our meal with much polite chat – but when it comes to the business at hand he nods, but not enthusiastically. He smiles the smile of man who does not want to disappoint his sons, but his heart is clearly not in the new venture. His body language says his enthusiasm for a deal is missing. He's polite, his arms folded, there's no real eye contact, and he has long private conversations with his wife. It's a crucial time in the negotiation, when the lack of a personal rapport is hindering progress. I'm keen to close this deal and so decide to tell this family story.

'Ah, I must tell you. My grandmother was born in Buenos Aires.' The grand old man listens politely to the translator.

'Tell us more,' says his translator.

'She was christened in a local church after her parents emigrated to Argentina to start a new life.' After a pause for the translation, *el padre* smiles a real smile for the first time, this time with his pale blue eyes.

'My grandmother's father robbed a bank in Liverpool and that night he boarded a boat to South America to start a new life with his wife. He bought a ranch near Buenos Aires and my grandma was born two years later. Unfortunately, when she was just two her father was murdered, shot by the local gauchos. His widow then returned to the UK with her daughter, my gran. They set up home in the north end of Birkenhead. It's all true.' It's an oft-told family story but I have missed out the bit where we have no hard evidence.

He waits patiently for the translation and then looks across the table and his smile lights up his entire face. His body language loosens. He gets up from his chair and walks around the large table. I stand up to greet him, and he shakes my hand until it almost falls off. '*El bandido*,' he says with a huge grin. The deal is sealed.

Recent research into my family's history has clarified this story. The bank robber has turned out to be one Mr George Turner, the father of my paternal gran. She was born Georgina Florence Turner in Argentina. It turns out he did not rob a bank at all. He was the clerk to a corrupt Liverpool solicitor who ran money-lending scams and cheque fraud. His boss, one Harry Sidney Hanchett Rennolls, was charged with a £1,000 cheque fraud. In today's money that's £115,000. When the law closed in on the fraud and charged both the corrupt solicitor and his clerk, George turned king's evidence against his boss in a plea bargain. Immediately after the trial he fled the country, knowing full well that the heavies used by his boss to enforce his loan shark deals would be on his tail. He chose to go to Argentina with his wife to start a new life. We think he chose Buenos Aires rather than New York as it would have been more difficult for the heavies to track him down in South America. But there is no record on any sailings of George Turner as a passenger and, given that he knew his pursuers could easily get hold of passenger lists, it is likely he worked his passage: as anonymous crew he would be safe from scrutiny. On Gran's birth certificate in 1891 his trade is down as shipping clerk. His wife returned to the UK with Georgina when she was ten years old, not two as in the family story, and without George. He had not been shot. He had died of typhoid fever.

9

FOOTBALL, GIRLS, RHYTHM 'N' BLUES BANDS

When we aren't watching nature there are other life forms to observe, scrutinise and enjoy. It's 1960 and I'm a 13-year-old when my mate Dave takes me to a football game. We choose the big club, Everton. (Liverpool FC is a minnow, mired in the second division. It has just appointed a new manager by the name of William Shankly.) We travel to Walton by train, taking one under the Mersey, then another to Kirkdale.

The walk to the ground takes us through Walton, where long streets of terraced houses belch sooty smoke, and kids play with their own scuffed leather football. If you're lucky, goalposts are marked on a wall in chalk, but more often goals are jackets and coats piled up in the road. The few cars that pass are expected to dodge any temporary goalposts. Thin clothes lines cross the street at roof height, strung with working denim blues and off-white washing. A few ladies scrub their steps and chat to their neighbours. There's a community here, just like my own street.

We come to the end of a terrace, and the shuffling fans turn right towards the ground. And there is my first sight of the main stand of Goodison Park. A slanting, pale blue corrugated roof rises like a huge sunbird with wings spread out, shading lines of terraced roofs. Local pubs are busy, spilling their patrons out into the street. At major crossroads there are four pubs, one on each corner. The chip shops are doing well.

Lines of blue and white-scarfed supporters merge into hundreds. Slowly they enter the ground through the many clunking-tight, iron turnstiles. We look at our ticket for our own turnstile number, find our entrance in the main stand, go to the back of the queue, and when it's our turn show the ticket to the attendant, who lets us in with his hidden foot pedal. A heavy click and the turnstile takes my forward push and clanks locked behind me. We're in, we made it.

Dark, poorly lit cavernous brick halls offer pies, beer and gents' urinals. Rising steps, dimly lit by the light filtering in, lead up to the terraces. Climb the steps and enter the arena. Towering floodlights at all four corners of the ground illuminate a massive wall of blue and white double-decker stands filled with chanting fans. The shout 'Ev-er-ton, Ev-er-ton, Ev-er-ton!' rings clear. Guys with wooden rattles, clackers, make their presence felt. A few police officers patrol.

As wee lads, we go to the front so we can have an unobstructed view. The floor is damp; it must have been raining when we were coming here. We are up against the white concrete wall, just a few feet from the pitch. It's a good half-hour before kick-off; time to look around. The green pitch in front us has muddy patches, especially near the two goals. I'm surprised that the pitch is not flat: I can't see the far touch line, as it's hidden by the playing surface's slightly convex curve.

With 30 minutes to go before kick-off, a lady walks around the pitch near the touchline; she's dressed in blue, including a bonnet and a full-length frilly skirt. From her wicker basket she is showering the crowd with sweets. Everton Toffees, I am told. She walks the perimeter, chucking her toffees high into the crowd. On the opposite touchline display boards carry all the letters of the alphabet. I will learn their purpose at half time.

The crowd behind us grows. Cast-iron crash barriers begin to do their work, holding up and separating the enormous crowd. A work-worn, heavy hand on my shoulder shoves me to one side, and a big bear of a bloke takes my place against the white wall. He relieves himself, but he shows commendable decorum as he rolls up his pink *Echo* and uses it as a funnel to piss through. I notice he takes his paper with him as he leaves. He calmly says, 'Thanks, laa.' I feel better. Lesson number one: the white front wall also doubles as a urinal for those in need. Arrggh! The damp floor!

It's not long to kick-off, and the frisson is tangible. We are near the halfway line, not far from where the players come onto the pitch. They appear to a huge roar. My eyes are parallel with their knees. I can almost touch them. One Everton player stubs out a fag, and it doesn't seem odd. Our players turn toward the high banking of the Gladwys Street end, and a local tells me the crowd here is worth a goal: 'They've been known to draw breath and *suck* the ball into the net.' Dave buys a programme for threepence, and we slowly put names to the numbers on the players' backs. We are playing Chelsea. Their colours are also blue and white, but today, as the away team, they have turned out in their bright canary yellow away strip with blue numbers on their backs.

Although there's plenty of hustling, bruising contact on the pitch, my first impression is one of sheer athletic strength and skill, especially from the forwards. One guy stands out – Alex Young. Balletic feet and poise. The Golden Vision. A small guy who dribbles effortlessly and drifts past defenders. Then Brian Labone, our centre half and captain, is a colossus. Crunch tackles are flying in, but the crowd are incensed by the constant fouling by a stocky Chelsea half-back, by the name of Ron 'Chopper' Harris.

At half time, stewards in white coats bring out white metal plates roughly one foot square with numbers in black. They hook these metal plates either side of the letters on the far side of the pitch. Another guy does a similar job on the letters on our side of the pitch, but of course we can't read these. From the programme we gather that each letter corresponds to a game currently in play, as all First Division games kick off at the same time, 3.00 pm. The numbers either side of the letter give the half-time score. Thereafter, as the scores change the stewards alter the numbers.

Full time arrives. We have won 4–0, with a brace of goals from the Golden Vision himself, Alex Young, and one each from Derek Temple and Roy Vernon. A memorable, magic day. We go home enthused and pick up the evening's *Echo* to read the match report. The visit had started as a casual suggestion by another birdwatcher, and little do I know that I'm hooked for life.

You would think, after all life throws at you, that football would play a minor role in the activities of a reasonably well-educated adult – but no, even now, 60-plus years later, it is a tangibly evocative experience for me to relive my first ever visit to Goodison Park, the grand old stadium, back at the age of 13. My very own winter migration to a piece of green turf, like those purple sandpipers on the rocks of New Brighton. I still make my first visit of the season to my seat in Upper Bullens before the end of August, and it's May before we have our final match.

I would have been in my late thirties when I went to see the Toffees in a home game. I parked in a side street and a lad on his little push bike, no more than six or seven years old, rode up when I was getting out of the car: 'Mind your car, mister?'

I paid him 20p: 'You look after it and I'll give you another 20p when I get back.'

That day we won the league when we beat Spurs 1–0,[29] and I was late leaving, consuming both the atmosphere and a beer or two. When I returned to collect my car, the street was empty. Mine was the only car left. I got in and turned on the engine. Suddenly there was a knock on the driver's window by a young black kid, again no more than six or seven. I wound the window down. We were staring at each other face to face, a gap of just 9 inches.

'You promised another 20p,' he said.

'I did – but you're not the lad I left to look after my car.'

'That's orright; he's given us the franchise.'

I still chuckle at that story. I hope he made it out of the back streets of Walton.

These days, the walk across Stanley Park sees families decked in blue with the name of their favourite player on their shirts bought from Everton 1, the merchandise store at the ground. The club has opened a second merchandise store, Everton 2. It's in the new shopping precinct, called Liverpool 1. A neat address.

It's all seating today, so no crush barriers or massive, swaying crowds. It's safer, but the crowd is only 40,000. Nowadays the *Z Cars* theme rips out on the tannoys as the players enter the fray and cross that sacred white line. But there is still the excited walk to the ground, the smell of the chippie, big guys drinking their pints outside local pubs and then, at last, the loud clunk of the turnstile lock. The walk up the steps into the Upper

---

29   That was 11 May 1987. We won the First Division, as it was then, title by nine points from a team from across the park whose name escapes me. Our squad was made up of seventeen English players, three Welsh lads, including Neville Southall, who with Gordon Banks can be considered the best goalkeepers I have ever seen, two Scots, and one guy from Northern Ireland with a great left foot, Kevin Sheedy.

Bullens stand still carries the expectant thrill of all the bright colours of the green pitch, the players' strips and the blue and white decorated stands. I have been blessed: I have enjoyed a good decade of games with the company of one of my daughters. She started as an 11-year-old, two years younger than me when I went to my first game.

I'm there to feed not on meat and potato pies but on hope: a win in a style as befits the School of Soccer Science. I'm there to nourish my roots with affection and pride. I'm there to be caught in the soft safety net of tribal belonging.

Popular culture is not only football. Beat groups are everywhere. It seems each street has a group or a band of three guitars – the musicians – and a drummer. (A tad unfair, perhaps, to drummers?) The port of Liverpool is home to many cellar clubs where the main offer of jazz now involves rhythm 'n' blues. Live Liverpool bands play their own version of many American standards like 'Kansas City', 'Some Other Guy' and 'Twist & Shout'. This is the new Beat scene. Jazz has a long, strong hold in Liverpool, but this is different. A musical extension, but with more sex and energy. The Beatles' first hit, 'Love Me Do', is released in October 1962. It never makes number one – but boy, does it generate a feeling of belonging: local and special. Liverpool is just across the Mersey from Leasowe; accents are similar, and bands play both sides of the river, even our left bank.

Getting to Liverpool to listen to these bands is a risky business for us young teenagers; the last train home, the last ferry, are too dangerous. Fully kitted teddy-boy gangs prowl. So we go to the Kraal in New Brighton. This club, in the cellars of a big old house, is just down from the Floral Pavilion, the local music hall theatre. There is a back way in, avoiding the guys who want cash on the door, but it is fraught. Shards of broken bottle glass set in cement line the top of 6-foot walls.

'How did you get this rip in your trousers?' my mum asks.

'Ar, ay, Ma, I dunno.'

Curved arched cellar ceilings drip sweat from pulsating young bodies dancing to whatever band is playing. The Kraal is alive, packed and hot. Glamorous girls swivel their hips and look magnificent in their back-combed bee-hive hairdos. Us boys sidle in for a dance. Gone are the formalities of askin'. A smile is enough to know she doesn't mind.

But when she turns her back on you and continues to dance with her mates around their small clutch of handbags carefully piled up on the floor, you know you have no chance.

The place is busy to bursting and it's difficult to move, but the scene is intoxicating. Everyone is packed tight. Unlike those more formal dances in local halls where girls dance on one side of the hall and boys gather on the other as a DJ plays the current hit parade.

Denis and I go along and try our luck at such a dance at the West Kirby Sailing Club. West Kirby is possibly out of our league. Posh totty. But hey, the organisers take our money and there's no questions asked as we gulp our under-age pints. I see a cracker on the other side of the hall, and a pint of Watney's Red Barrel has worked wonders for my courage. There's a decent Chuck Berry number playing, and I cross the hall's empty divide and ask a slim, long-haired blonde for a dance. She takes one look and delivers her all too swift put-down. Perhaps I aimed too high. The walk back across that empty hall takes forever.

Denis smirks and suggests, 'She's after older guys.'

'But I put my long trousers on especially, and I've been shaving now for three years.'

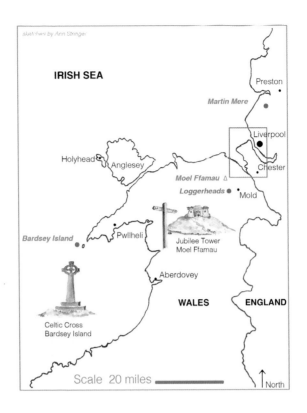

sketches by Ann Stringer

IRISH SEA

Preston

Martin Mere

Liverpool

Holyhead   Anglesey

Chester

Moel Ffamau △

Loggerheads ●   Mold

Bardsey Island   Pwllheli

Jubilee Tower
Moel Ffamau

Aberdovey

WALES   **ENGLAND**

Celtic Cross
Bardsey Island

Scale 20 miles ▬▬▬▬   ↑ North

sketches by Ann Stringer

Fort Perch Rock
New Brighton

Anglican Cathedral
Liverpool

New Brighton

Leasowe

Meols

Red Rocks

Hilbre Isles

Leasowe Lighthouse

West Kirby

The Boat House
Hilbre

Thingwall ●

Mersey
Basin

Dee Estuary

The Wirral

Parkgate ●

Burton Marshes ●

Scale 4 miles ▬▬▬   ↑ North

[Photo 1] Red kite, Mid Walzes, August 2015
'Red kites hang in updraughts and look for carrion.'

[Photo 2] Blue tit, the Wirral, August 2015

'The little blue and yellow bird … is a blue tit.'

[Photo 3] Black-headed gull, Cheshire, October 2020

'The white leading edge to their wings contrasts sharply with the dark cloud backdrop.'

[Photo 4] Curlew, Meols, April 2018

'Larger birds, like oystercatcher and curlew, fly directly over our heads, making for the meadows to feed.'

[Photo 5] Sanderling, Red Rocks, Hoylake, March 2021

*'A group of three sanderling feed together in the soft early morning
light, just where the tide's limit refreshes the sharp shell sand.'*

[Photos 6 and 7] Snow buntings, North Wales, January 2017
'A couple of snow buntings feed on the seed heads of wild grass stems.'

[Photo 8] Redwing, Spurn Point, March 2018

[Photo 9] Fieldfare, Leighton Moss, Nov 2016

'There is more activity in the lanes as continental redwing and fieldfare join the local blackbird population to strip berries from rowan and hawthorn.'

[Photo 10] Redshank, Red Rocks, Hoylake, February 2018
'Redshank in frozen snow scour the mudflats for morsels.'

[Photo 11] Skylark, Leasowe, March 2018
'Ethereal minstrel! pilgrim of the sky!'

[Photo 12] Male stonechat, Leasowe, March 2018

'His black head, like a hood, extends down to his chin and nape.'

[Photo 13] Female stonechat, Leasowe, March 2018

'The nearby female, in her duller plumage, pays little attention and keeps a low profile in the bracken.'

[Photos 14 and 15] Leasowe Lighthouse, January 2021

'Leasowe lighthouse is a short walk from the common; it lies empty, locked, derelict and technically in Moreton.'

[Photo 16] Raven, Isle of Lewis, May 2017
*'Their massive heads and beaks and bright dark
shiny eyes give them an ominous look.'*

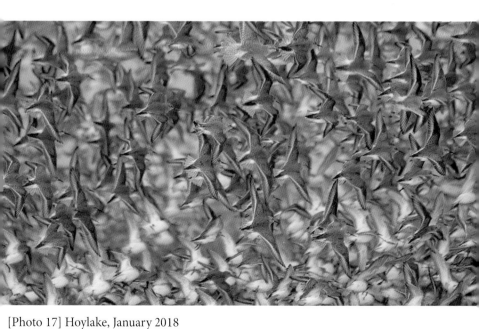

[Photo 17] Hoylake, January 2018
'The flock gets the jitters over a passing falcon and a section takes to the air.'

[Photo 18] Redshank, Hoylake, January 2018

'A single, confident redshank takes flight, away from the throng.'

[Photo 19] Kestrel hovering, Leasowe, March 2018

'A lone kestrel hovers against the wind then dips for the kill but returns unrewarded to patrol the next sector of sunken meadow.'

[Photo 20] Hilbre's islands, August 2017

Looking back to the Wirral from Hilbre Island at high tide towards Middle Hilbre and Little Eye.

[Photo 21] Hilbre Island, August 2017

'Red sandstone has been eroded by wind.'

[Photo 22] Hilbre Island
The old boathouse.

[Photo 23] Dunlin, Hilbre Island, August 2017
'Many wading birds have this feature, called distal rhynchokinesis …
ryncho is an upper mandible, kinesis means movement, and distal
means 'far from the point of attachment', in this case the end of the bill.
It's a long name for what is simply a flexible end to the top mandible.'

[Photo 24]
Redshank, Hoylake,
January 2018
*'A redshank is
caught, backlit in the
setting sun's focused
bright light.'*

[Photo 25] Purple sandpiper, North Uist, May 2021
*'Of all the waders feeding on the rocky shoreline during an incoming tide,
the stout purple sandpipers are the last to abandon a favourite feeding
spot, clinging to wave-splashed, seaweed-covered boulders.'*

[Photo 26] New Brighton Lighthouse, September 2020
'As the tide begins to ebb, wave-worn lines of dark-brown sandstone begin to show near New Brighton's Perch Rock lighthouse.'

[Photo 27] Short-eared owl, Parkgate, March 2020

'She is still there as dusk descends.'

[Photo 28] Dipper, Derbyshire, February 2021

'The dipper is off upstream, carrying a caddis fly larva shell, her wings whirring.'

[Photo 29] Spotted flycatcher, Spain, June 2019

'One of these birds lifts off from its favourite perch, catches a nearby flying insect and returns to the same shaded perch to feast. There's a clue in its name.'

[Photo 30] Pink-footed geese, Martin Mere, October 2019

'The outriders leading this dark grey silhouetted blizzard of geese start to descend. The scouts must know there are many more behind, so wherever they choose has to be right.'

[Photo 31] Pink-footed geese, Leasowe, January 2021

'The chevron-shaped flying formation works to the flocks mutual advantage…… each trailing bird on either side of the leader gets help from the bird in front, each one behind meeting with less wind resistance.'

[Photo 32] Whooper swans, Martin Mere, November 2017

'We creep closer until we can go no further. Wild swans from Iceland. Whooper swans.'

[Photo 33] Barn owl, River Alt, Lancashire, July 2017

'The owl carries it in one claw and flaps off across the field back to the ditch, exactly where we are sitting, and gives us a long stare.'

[Photo 34] Bar-tailed godwit, Canary Islands, January 2020

'The bar-tailed godwits we see in Britain have a comparatively easy journey, setting off from northern Scandinavia and Russia on a course between west and south-west, with only the short North Sea crossing to contend with..'

[Photo 35] Fulmar, Bempton Cliffs, October 2019

'A fulmar passes overhead, silhouetted against the dark cliffs with stiff wings stretched out to collect every ounce of updraft.'

[Photo 36] Meadow pipit, Leasowe, August 2018

'A meadow pipit needs a quick check. Perched on a post with a beak full of insects. A second brood?'

[Photo 37] Linnet, Pembrokeshire, April 2017
'A parcel of linnets settle near the track ahead and feed off mature grass seed-heads.

[Photo 38] Bardsey Island, September 2020

'To the south the lighthouse is bathed in fresh clear light.
My eyes rest easy on this pleasant isle.'

[Photo 39] Northern Wheatear, Bardsey Island, April 2021

'A northern wheatear in black, silvery-grey and white livery sits nearby on a
boulder covered in ancient lichen. The orange of the lichen patches matches
the orangey-pink of the wheatear's throat feathers, ruffled by the breeze. Is he
interested in my laverbread? I tear off a piece and throw it in his direction.
His dark eyes inspect the morsel and then he looks at me. He decides I'm no
threat. I'm part of his world and he's part of mine. His white tail feathers
flash bright as he picks up a titbit and retreats to a safer distance.'

IO

SPARTINA

We agree to meet at Birkenhead's Woodside ferry terminal at 7.30 on a Saturday morning in late April. Colourful buses arrive by the minute, and ferries to Liverpool leave every 30, on the hour and half-hour. Birkenhead Corporation's buses have a pale royal blue and yellow trim; Wallasey Corporation's are swathed in their distinctive daffodil yellow. Crosville's buses ply their trade between various boroughs on the Wirral and North Wales in their shiny, dark olive green. Number F17, our Bristol-engined double-decker Crosville, waits at its allocated shelter.[30] The driver has scrolled through his list of destinations from his cab, and there it is, Parkgate, on the front display. A warm, empty bus. Pride of place is upstairs at the front.

Birders on Hilbre paint an exciting picture of what can be seen on the marshes around Parkgate, an old fishing village sitting neatly 10 miles upstream from West Kirby and Hilbre on the English side of the wide Dee Estuary. The attraction to naturalists is the vast salt marsh which stretches over to Wales. For me this is a new habitat, which means new species.

---

30   Crossville double-deckers were not as tall as the other buses at Woodside terminus. They were specifically designed to cope with the many low bridges carrying railway lines. When you climbed the stairs under the sign 'No Spitting Upstairs' you then walked along a single sunken corridor on the right-hand side of the upper deck, which gave you access to six or seven bench seats which stretched across the width of the bus. Each seat could carry at least four passengers. On the lower deck, headroom on the right-hand side was very limited due to the sunken walkway on the upper one.

The bus starts up and slowly climbs away from Woodside, heading south for Rock Ferry. Our upper deck seats offer good views. Chaffinches socialise in small flocks amongst hawthorn blossom; house sparrows squabble in tall hedges; a moorhen bobs its way across an inundated field. Mallard dabble at the flood's margins. A hen blackbird raises her tail upright and flicks her wings as she lands on a branch; jackdaws cavort and play.

After 40 minutes, F17 trundles down a gentle gradient from Neston to Parkgate, journey's end. She finally pulls up on a small square off the long, straight sandstone promenade, which has also acted as a busy quayside in a previous life.

On our left is the marsh, 8 to 10 feet below the level of the road. On our right, rows of old fishermen's cottages sit tight to the kerb, with not even room for a decorative flowerpot. A few slipways off the promenade recall the days when the tide would come up to the cottages. Rusted metal rings fixed into what was the quay's wall hark back to Parkgate's shrimping days, and before them the Parkgate Packets, which had provided a well-established ferry service to Dublin (more on this in Chapter 12).

Salt marsh stretches across the wide estuary. High cloud and patches of blue sky from the west suggest a clear day ahead. A line of rotting, mustard-coloured vegetation, 6 feet in width, has settled on the marsh close to the road, brought in several months ago by an exceptionally high spring tide. A freshwater drainage gulley trickles from a culvert under the road. Tall yellowing spartina, or cordgrass, borders a few tidal ditches and brackish pools. Early flowering purple sea lavender and yellow sea asters add colour. The high marsh covers a vast area stretching out for a mile: a haven for wildlife, from voles to harriers, redshank to merlin and teal to pinkfeet.

High tide arrives slowly and unseen, surreptitiously filling creeks and channels, ditches and dykes. A few saltpans dot the near landscape, dark pools of sea water still visible at low tide. An ideal spot to find patches of glasswort or samphire.

Beyond the high marsh, where regular tides ebb and flow, lines of redundant fence posts cross this flat wetland mosaic. Sheep graze on soft, dark green turf: salt marsh lamb, a local delicacy.

A lone, stray Friesian looks out of place out there on the distant, pastoral turf.

A few miles to the south, near Shotton, filthy yellow clouds of sulphurous steam belch from the blackened stacks of the sprawling John Summers Iron and Steel Works. Fellow birders tell of what can be seen out there, near its man-made causeway of coke and clinker. We share the OS map and pore over its detail. Our day needs to be planned carefully; there is only one bus back, early in the evening.

We tread south, keeping to the shoreline, and make our way along ditches with little regard for the law of trespass, persuading ourselves if we do no damage we cannot be prosecuted.

We hear the guns of wildfowlers letting rip. 'Aren't they supposed to pack their guns away during the breeding season?' asks Bob.

Mac spots a lone ringtail harrier out on the marsh. He thinks it's a female hen harrier. It's late April, and we can't make out any of the yellowy underside colouring that would suggest an immature bird. She hunts by surprise low over the marshes, her long wings providing uplift after occasional flaps, her head peering down at 90 degrees from her body, looking for prey. Her tail, a rudder, dictates a deliberate, quartering search pattern. Her white rump, or ringtail, flashes as she twists and turns. Occasionally she drops into the sedge but soon reappears to continue her patrol. She's here for the last of her spring days. Her usual summer patch is high in the Welsh mountain moors, where she breeds.

A few family skeins of wild geese, pinkfeet, offer a last glimpse of their restlessness. Most have already left for Iceland. A water rail squeals like a wounded pig from a nearby reed bed. Is that a merlin we see on a far fence post?

After an hour's slow tramp along the edges of the high marsh, we close in on the vast steel works, like metal insects drawn magnetically towards the noisy giant, many-headed, carnivore beast of the roaring blast furnaces. Are we too close? We see the faces of the men in their bright orange boiler suits working on high gantries.

The guys on Hilbre had told us, 'When you get near the clinker causeway, look out for the tell-tale signs of rising vapours of cooling effluent.' These rectangular pools of burnt orange, sulphurous yellow and silty-brown acrid effluent attract wildlife which warrants close inspection. We try to keep upwind, as we might choke on their filthy fumes. We are surely now trespassing big-time, but a higher priority is that we want to detect birds whilst remaining undetected. We crawl along ditches and jump drains.

Our reward is an incongruous birders' mecca. A couple of small, rare waders which go by the titles of little stint and curlew sandpiper. There's also little gull, whimbrel and green sandpiper. How can this be, this bizarre paradox? All this exotic birdlife amidst industrial man's crud and grunge. How does that work?

Finding a suitable spot on the causeway, we take lunch and make sure we stay hidden. Mac, Bob, Roy and me. It's time to scribble in our notebooks and start the count. Being noble purists, we have set targets for the day: 50 species would be good, 75 brilliant. We have come to see new birds, and we're doing just that. New birds bring new discussions. Where do they migrate to and when? What are the bird's plumage variations between sexes, or sexual dimorphism, to give the condition its scientific terminology? How about their songs and calls, nesting sites and habits? Conversations are sporadic, intent and brief as we keep watch. We look for patterns, similarities with other species. We search for credible explanations. Knowledge accumulates like individual autumn leaves slowly falling onto the sunlit floor of a woodland dell. We understand more, and there's more to come. Facts accrue. Opinions gel. As we discover these wild places, lasting friendships form.

Roy checks his watch. Plenty of time to return to Parkgate. We leave the causeway and its pungent pools, and head back, slightly quicker this time. We bimble through the boggy edges of the high marsh, climb a few muddy banks and stumble across another old sandstone quay near Burton. It's time for a rest. We sit in a line with our feet dangling over a 6-foot drop to the soft quagmire below.

Mac does a quick count from his notebook. 'Sixty-eight so far today, not bad at all.' His tone reflects a modest self-content.

A moorhen jerks across the saltpan, a teal upends and dabbles in the shallows. Dunlin feed in the margins.

Ten yards away, a few teal, redshank and busy dunlin feed. Soft bog stretches 50 yards out to where high spartina begins. Green shoots show in contrast to the ochre colours of worn-out cordgrass, standing 4 feet tall, rippling in gentle unison to the embrace of a soft southerly breeze.

Beyond the high marsh we see those same beguiling Welsh hills, lit by the afternoon's high sun, now fazed to gentle soft blues.

A peregrine falcon skims silently close by, just a few feet above ground. Powerful, thrusting wingbeats hurl the bird forward. For a moment she is at head height between us and the high marsh. Slate-blue back and dark wings glint in the afternoon sun before she suddenly rises high in the warm sky, returning to where she belongs.

Her scythe-like wings cut sickle shapes in thin air. She wheels and turns until she is higher still, now a black dot. Her Horus eyes must clearly see her tiny prey below. She holds the sky close. She waits.

Several dunlin are busy preening, spreading lanolin to protect their feathers. The salt marsh sits soft and unnoticed whilst the falcon surveys. The sun's soothing light lifts out the yellows of the fading cordgrass stalks.

She fixes her sights on the group of birds, adjusting her height slightly to gauge the distance of the stoop she is considering. Her trained brain says 'go'. She folds her wings tight to her body and dives, like an accelerating slingshot. The teal are the first to take flight, followed by the redshank. Within metres of the kill she thrusts out her yellow talons as the dunlin take flight – too late. Her momentum takes out a dunlin by breaking a wing. She's chosen the weakest spot, as the shock of hitting a heavy body at speed could harm her.

She grabs the frail, broken wader. In her contrasting languid flight, she severs the wader's spinal cord using the jagged tomial tooth on her upper mandible, and the dunlin is now a warm, lifeless carcass. She finds a favourite spot to devour her meal. A grassy knoll which stands a foot proud of the marsh. Predator and prey in a final embrace. She tears at the breast, her bobbing head ripping out the feathers into a spray of white around the kill. She stops for a second to look both ways, and then continues with that head action. Red flesh rips and ruptures from the white breastbone.

She's soon had her fill. Time to recoil to the sky, leaving just a tell-tale trace of bones, quills, plumes and blood – dunlins are, after all, small birds – on her knoll.

A moorhen jerks across the saltpan, a teal upends and dabbles in the shallows. One fewer dunlin feed in the margins.

Here the peregrine falcon is queen of all she surveys, another apex predator. The larger female bird is the falcon; the male, the tiercel, is two-thirds her size, more slender, more agile, if that's possible.

The only limit on the numbers of peregrines breeding here is food supply. Their only predatory threat are foxes, who will try to take their eggs or chicks if the parent birds build their nest close to the ground. But those out hunting on the marsh will be nesting in safe nearby quarries and cliff faces, likely to be in those distant hills of North Wales. We see another peregrine, another falcon.

'She looks like a different bird,' says Mac. 'Are there two breeding pairs?'

'Looks like,' I reply.

The falcon and tiercel will mate for life. They will hold onto their territories and use as many as five or six different nesting scrapes, mostly on cliff faces. Three to four eggs are common, incubation is around 30 days, and only her ladyship, the falcon, incubates at night.

The scientific name *falco peregrinus* and the English name 'peregrine falcon' translates as the wandering falcon, a name commonly used in Asia, referring to their migratory habits. The species is widespread in every land mass on this planet barring New Zealand and the polar regions: in the Arctic the peregrine is replaced by the gyrfalcon, a mighty hunter in monochrome.

The western light over the Welsh hills is fading now, just as dusk begins to cast its black shawl over to the east. We hear the cackle of geese heading off north to breed. It is time, too, for us to head back to Parkgate for our own northerly route, by Crossville bus to Birkenhead.

'What's that noise in the rushes?' asks Bob.

'Could be Moses?' says Roy, ever the one for a quip.

Bob picks up the excited, rasping call of a sedge warbler from within an overgrown reed bed. We wait for it to climb the shrub before we see this smart little warbler. It will have arrived very recently, perhaps overnight, from sub-Saharan Africa.[31]

Noisy rooks begin to roost in high trees by the marsh's edge. A couple of sparring jays break out from a copse to carry on their skirmish. The

---

31   Recent ringing records have shown that sedge warblers can cover immense distances in a very short time. One made the Saharan crossing in 24 hours. No doubt accompanied by a following wind.

fracas is likely to be over food; jays are one of the few bird species who carefully cache their acorn larder. But it's spring. Another 100 yards and we are back on the promenade. We make it in time. Our warm, cosy Crossie waits.

'A shortie,' one of us whispers.

'Yes, a shortie! A big bird, probably female,' says Mac.

The day is not over. Just as we climb the ten steps on the slipway from the marsh to the promenade, we spot an owl, just 10 yards out, flying towards us. The bird follows the course of a hidden ditch. Her flight is placid and slow; a silent, bouncy, floppy affair. She is just a few feet above the marsh when she detects something, probably a vole. She dives head first into the cordgrass. She soon reappears, preyless, and continues her patrol. She settles on a bare tree stump and starts to preen. A sure sign she is not unsettled by our presence.

Short-eared owls are so called because of a couple of feather tufts which they raise as a defence mechanism when they feel threatened. These tufts look like mammalian ears but are no such thing. Our bird is not showing these tufts but everything else is there, especially the big head with its large white facial disk. Those piercing, formidable yellow eyes stare at us. Her bill is heavily hooked. Her upperparts dark mottled brown, her underparts soft white, her upper breast heavily streaked in brown arrowheads. She is magnificent, and stares at us with a look of mild curiosity.

Roy checks his watch again. There's 100 yards to the bus. We could watch her for hours. One last look before we take our seats. She is still there as dusk descends. (*Photo 27*)

Westward, the blue Welsh hills are framed by the setting sun. New worlds of boggy moorlands, of heather and bracken, dark forests of spruce and larch, and swift-flowing rivers of clean, clear water. There's a distant mountain which has a squat, castle-like structure on its summit. Bob says it's called Moel Ffamau. Is it the romantic setting sun which once again stirs our thoughts of new places, identities and language?

Checking the OS map we discover that the dotted line near John Summers, the iron and steel works, is the boundary between Wales and England. We have just crossed that imaginary line, the Welsh border. But now we want to explore deeper into Wales and unearth its mysteries in those magnificent distant hills.

11

FARMERS, PLEASE STOP USING DDT!

Attitudes to the environment have changed dramatically since we first heard those wildfowlers' shotguns out on the Parkgate marshes in April in the early sixties. There was indignation at the time, but little else stirred in the conservation world. The only environmental issues of note were warnings not to go swimming off certain public beaches such as those at Blackpool, due to the presence of untreated sewage. When the John Summers Steelworks was built at Shotton on the Dee Estuary's marshes, little thought would have been given to the impact on the environment.

It was around this time, September 1962, that Rachel Carson's seminal work, *Silent Spring*, was published.[32] Her volume was the first popular book to expose and protest against the damage done to our environment by the indiscriminate agricultural use of man-made chemicals. The theme of her book was that the use of sprayed DDT (dichloro-diphenyl-trichloroethane, an organochlorine compound), killed off wildlife. She was vilified not only by the public relations outfits hired by the chemical company which produced DDT, but also by colleagues in academia. In at least one case it got personal: the fact she was attractive but single apparently made her 'a communist'. So said former US Secretary of Agriculture Ezra Taft Benson in a letter to former US President Dwight D. Eisenhower.

---

32 Rachel Carson's *Silent Spring* was first published in 1962. In 2006 the editors of *Discover* magazine named it one of the 25 greatest science books of all time.

We owe her a lot. Even if her contribution to the environmental movement earned her comparatively little recognition in her own lifetime – she died less than two years after the publication of *Silent Spring*, so the controversy it had aroused was still raging – there have been many posthumous awards and honours, local, national and international, that commemorate her. She even had a pop song commemorating her work: 'Big Yellow Taxi', a track off the *Ladies of the Canyon* album released by Joni Mitchell in 1970.[33]

When we were tramping the marshes at Parkgate as youngsters, we were unaware that peregrines, our local apex predator, had already suffered from the effects of DDT spraying. By 1964, 80 per cent of the UK peregrine population had been lost. Only birds in the remoter parts of the Scottish Highlands, where DDT was not used, were unaffected. Peregrines on the Parkgate marsh escaped lightly, as there was no reason to use the chemical. DDT was an arable farmer's pest control tool, so it would not have been used on the Wirral and in North Wales.

DDT kills insects known to carry malaria and typhus, so it appeared to be beneficial to humans, but its indiscriminate use on crops and livestock was not understood at all. Organochlorines entered the food chain via mice and voles feeding off sprayed crops. Organochlorines are not excreted but build up in fatty tissues, leading to pesticide biomagnification further up the food chain. When raptors eat wildlife killed by DDT, the organochlorines slowly accumulate in their own fatty tissues. This in turn leads to lower levels of calcium in eggshells, which dramatically reduces successful hatching, as the eggshells easily break. This shell-thinning, together with increased adult mortality from ingestion, led to a catastrophic drop in peregrine numbers. DDT had the same effect on the populations of kestrels and buzzards.

DDT was developed in the 1940s, the first of the modern synthetic insecticides. It was banned in the US in 1972 – but it took another 12

---

33 If Joni Mitchell does it for you, there's a lovely book by Malka Marom called *Joni Mitchell, Both Sides Now*, which I heartily recommend. Malka was asked to interview Joni Mitchell in 1973. She accepted, and more conversations followed, and this book was published in 2014. It's a glossy coffee-table production with great artwork and much emphasis on the poetry in her lyrics and a collection of her paintings. It's written in dialogue form between the author and J.M., covering her life's ups and downs through relationships, the creative music process and gigs like Woodstock, but the thread is the lyricism and poetry of her music. It's a tome to dip into and out of as your mood takes you.

years before the UK got around to a ban. Today, peregrine, kestrel and buzzard numbers have returned to where we were before DDT, but it is still patchy; and please don't think all is now fine for peregrines and other raptors, as there is a strong, statistically significant, correlation between poor breeding success of all our raptor community and those areas of the country, especially in Scotland and Wales, where landowners use the moors for their hugely profitable red grouse shoots. It is illegal to poison or shoot raptors. A few enlightened landowners do respect the law, but the figures speak for themselves.

It is a difficult one to pin down. Hard, incontrovertible evidence is difficult to come by, and prosecutions are rare. A bird of prey found shot is one thing. Getting a successful prosecution is another. 'Not me, M'lud; it must have flown in – shot by a scruffy scoundrel, no doubt – and the poor thing died on our land.'

In nature's balanced ecology our local apex predators, the magnificent peregrine, poses no threat. The same can't be said of our own species' evolutionary ascent to this pinnacle. The development of language and communication has trumped the need for the fiercest talons, the sharpest incisors and the fastest legs; we out-think and outsmart the most ferocious lions, bears and tigers. We are now the apex predator on our globe, and the hard, woeful, unremitting evidence tells us we are using this position to inflict untold damage on our environment.

We organise and exploit the world we live in, and have done so since we ceased to be hunter-gatherers and became settled agriculturalists producing a food surplus which could be stored for winter consumption or traded for other goods. Agriculture first appeared 12,000 years ago, give or take 1,000 years.[34]

Homo sapiens has been on the planet for around 200,000 years, plus or minus 5,000. During the last 12,000 years we have settled down in particular places, planted arable crops and herded sheep, goats, pigs and cattle. Although there is evidence that from the start of that time *Homo sapiens* was already

---

34 Agriculture appeared more or less simultaneously in several unconnected groups located in Asia, South America, Europe and the Middle East. In the West, we tend to think agriculture started in the 'fertile crescent' around the rivers Tigris and Euphrates in what is now Syria and Iraq, but this is not the whole story. Agriculture is another example of how important evolutionary changes are likely to occur simultaneously across non-connected populations.

altering the balance of nature by killing off the largest wild animals,[35] it's in the last 50 years that we have wreaked real havoc on our planet. This is due to the damage we are causing with the widespread use of toxic chemicals, carbon emissions from our use of fossil fuels and methane emissions from our overpowering numbers of ruminants, and the industrialisation of ever more invasive intensive agriculture, with the resulting loss of biodiversity. Not to mention other hazards such as mankind's growing resistance to antibiotics, nuclear proliferation and pollution by plastic. More recently there is dramatic evidence that the chemical residues of many items used in our lifestyle are making our own species increasingly infertile.

Although a few political decision-makers may be aware of what they're doing, the vast majority of humanity have not a clue about the effect of all but a few of their actions. How many, for example, are aware that their clothes made of polyester, acrylic etc are a major cause of pollution in the air and in the sea not just in their manufacture and disposal but also each time they are put through a washing machine? How many are aware that an empty bottle can become a deadly trap for hundreds of small creatures – or even, if the sun shines through it, start a wildfire?

We humans have overfished our oceans, destroyed bison in their millions for food or fun, killed off wolf packs to protect our farming livestock in both Europe and North America, and in the last 25 years destroyed 75 per cent of the UK's insect population. I could go on and on and on. The list of species destruction is devastating. Don't get me going on whales, big cats, elephants, rhinos and so on.

Humanity's impact on nature has been catastrophic – often, it must be said, the result of unintended consequences – whereas Nature, given a chance, will once again achieve her own ecological balance in which the interplay between species is complex, interdependent and rarely fully understood.

A much-cited example of the beneficial effect of apex predators on an ecosystem are the dramatic changes in Yellowstone National Park recorded after the grey wolf was reintroduced. Elk, the wolves' primary prey, had grown in numbers since 1926, when humans had hunted the grey wolf to extinction. The wolf's reintroduction in 1995 led to a decrease in elk numbers. This in turn led to behavioural changes in the surviving elk; as they

---

35   https://www.livescience.com/first-human-caused-animal-extinction.html

had become easy prey in their normal open riverside haunts they moved to more secluded country. As a result the riverside areas were saved from constant grazing, allowing willows, aspens (silver birch) and cottonwoods to flourish, creating habitats for beaver, moose and scores of other species.

The wolves' presence also had a positive effect on one of the park's most vulnerable species, the grizzly bear: emerging from hibernation, having fasted for months, bears can now scavenge recent wolf kills. More importantly, bears benefit from these kills in autumn, just as they are preparing to hibernate; as the grizzly gives birth during hibernation the numbers of surviving cubs has increased. Dozens of other species, including eagles, ravens, magpies, coyotes and black bears, have also been documented scavenging from wolf kills within the park.

This example is well known, but others, equally empirically valid, are to be found, and this has encouraged a programme of reintroduction together with a more informed management of the environment. At the time of writing, this is popularly referred to as 'rewilding'.

Nearer to home we have our own example of another apex predator which, like the wolf, used to be a threat to our agricultural practices. The white-tailed sea eagle used to roam freely around the UK, from Hampshire to the Shetland Isles. It's an inquisitive bird with few enemies – easily trapped and killed. Persecution, mainly by sheep farmers, ensured that the final UK population of the white-tailed sea eagle was extinct in Scotland by 1918, eight years before the wolf's similar demise in Yellowstone.

But then, from 1975 to 1985, 82 young Norwegian white-tailed sea eagles were reintroduced on the island of Rum. It turned out that the original birds cared little for Rum, but cared lots for neighbouring Mull, where they began to nest. It's a slow process, though. Even if a pair of birds successfully raise an eaglet or two, it takes another five years for the young birds to reach sexual maturity. This reintroduction was always going to take time. At first it was impossible to know whether reintroduction was a success. But after a few fits and starts, Scotland now has a burgeoning population of over 100 nesting pairs, mostly along the western coast. A success story. [36]

---

36 John A. Love has chronicled the reintroduction of the white-tailed sea eagle in his book *A Saga of Sea Eagles*, published by Whittles. John covered the 1985 Rum introduction of this majestic species in his book *The Return of The Sea Eagle*, and this new offer extends the original narrative. This is real time conservation in detail and at first hand.

This home-grown example of rewilding has not been without its ups and downs. The Scottish RSPB still gets calls from farmers saying, 'One of your eagles killed my lamb.' The farmer sees an eagle sitting on a dead lamb and naturally thinks the eagle has killed the lamb. But that may not be the case. Analysis of the remnants of kills at sea eagle nests suggests that eagles predate on many species including the odd lamb – but whether one would have taken a live, healthy lamb is another question. There is little hard evidence.

In May 2016, I took a boat trip out from Kallin in North Uist. We had the very good fortune to have a nesting sea eagle fly over our boat and take a fish thrown in by Nick, our skipper. He liaises with the RSPB to promote the tourist potential these birds bring to the Outer Isles, just as they have done on Mull and Skye. In this way the island communities see the wider benefits brought to them by these magnificent birds, with their huge 8-foot wingspan.

But the story does not end there. What has transpired is described in an edited extract from a blog by Roy Dennis in his Wildlife Foundation website, www.roydennis.org:

SEPTEMBER 1, 2019

It's now ten days since we released six juvenile White-tailed Eagles on the Isle of Wight. Each is equipped with a satellite transmitter that logs the bird's location once every three minutes, and this has given us a fascinating and very detailed insight into their movements since release. Five of the birds have remained at or close to the release site on the Isle of Wight, but one – G3 22 – has surprised us by making an incredible flight over central London to Essex. Research in Scotland and elsewhere has shown that juvenile White-tailed Eagles often wander widely in their first two years – often venturing 200km from their nest site. What we weren't expecting was for one of the Isle of Wight birds to do it within two weeks of release. It is testament to what good condition the bird is in.

G3 22 is a male from the North of the Island of Skye, and rather than refer to it by its ring number, we thought it good to choose an Isle of Wight/Solent name. So, we'll now be referring to G3 22 as 'Culver' – after Culver Cliff – the last place that White-tailed Eagles bred in southern England.

12

PARKGATE PACKETS

When I told Dad we had been birding at Parkgate, he explained that he had grown up just where the Crosville bus journey terminates, in a small fisherman's cottage on the southern edge of Parkgate's embankment: No. 1 The Cottage, South Promenade.

I recall his dad, my grandad George, sitting me on his knee, reciting the first two verses of 'The Sands of the Dee'. When it came to the repeating line, 'And call the cattle home', he would clasp his hand to his ear. His delivery carried a sinister, foreboding tone. The poem mourns the death of Mary, caught by the treacherous tides across the estuary when cattle were left to graze on the far-out marshes.

> O Mary, go and call the cattle home,
> And call the cattle home,
> And call the cattle home,
> Across the sands of Dee.
> The western wind was wild and dank with foam,
> And all alone went she.
> The western tide crept up along the sand,
> And o'er and o'er the sand,
> And round and round the sand,
> As far as eye could see.
> The rolling mist came down and hid the land:
> And never home came she.
>
> *Charles Kingsley, poet, and canon of Chester Cathedral (1819–1875)*

There's another unconfirmed family story, that George had claimed a reward for finding and bringing in a drowned body from these sands; but there is no hard evidence in the local papers. However, he did make the *Chester Chronicle* in 1917: a report from the Neston Petty Sessions finds George guilty of taking the train from Parkgate to Neston without a ticket 'with the intent to avoiding payment thereof'. The ticket would have cost him a penny farthing (1¼ pence). His fine was 15 shillings, 144 times as much. A gross penalty! Goodness knows how he managed to pay his fine. Perhaps he had to serve time?

Dad and his three brothers talked with great affection of Parkgate. Family stories, like the one of the four brothers sharing the one pair of shoes; the lad with the most difficult job, like leading horse carts on the cobbled streets, got the shoes. The four of them were in constant trouble with the local bobby, whether it was nicking orchard apples, breaking windows or the like. If there was any trouble the Parkgate Kendricks copped it. The four local scallies went off to war in France and the Pacific. All came back. All damaged in one way or other.

Our family hold dear a photograph, taken around 1929, of kids playing on a slipway in Parkgate, where the water laps the embankment. We have no idea who took this snap – but there they are, what we all take to be the four brothers and one sister, playing barefoot at high tide. A year earlier, in 1928, the community of Connah's Quay, on the Welsh bank of the Dee Estuary, decided to introduce *spartina anglica*, common cordgrass, to help prevent coastal erosion and to assist land reclamation. However, it is an invasive species and by the time of our visit as young birders, 30 years later in the early 1960s, *spartina* had colonised the entire mudflats across the River Dee.

It is difficult to imagine then, as it is now, that old Park Gate was once a thriving port on the principal passenger route from many parts of England to Dublin.

The tidal reach of the River Dee made Chester a viable and much used Roman port. But silting was a problem even as far back as the 4th century, when new quaysides had to be built downstream on the Cheshire side near Burton and Neston. By Georgian times these quaysides had become silted too, and a new quay was built where Neston's hunting park had its gates, hence the name Park Gate.

Park Gate became a busy port with regular services to Ireland and a ferry across the Dee Estuary to Bagillt in North Wales. By Georgian times Parkgate, as it became known, had become an important port of the north-west, especially for those wanting to get to and from Ireland. Most local folk know of the association of Parkgate and Neston with Lord Nelson. He was a frequent visitor to Parkgate, as Lady Emma Hamilton was from Ness, a local village. Earlier, in 1742, Handel had stayed there before he sailed to Dublin on the Parkgate Packet to conduct the first ever performance of The Messiah.

After the new cut had been made in 1737 to straighten and canalise the Dee from just below Chester to near Fflint, the deep navigable channel which used to run near the Wirral coast, with ports at Shotwick, Neston, Parkgate and Heswall, moved over to the Welsh side of the Dee estuary. Nature can be relentless, and further silting continued, which only helped to accelerate Parkgate's demise as a port – but fortunately in Victorian times Parkgate became a popular seaside destination, allowing visitors to enjoy what sands were left from the slowly encroaching salt marsh.

Very occasionally we still see tidal waters lap against Parkgate's embankment. Three meteorological conditions need to be present: a deep low pressure system, strong to gale force winds from the north or west, and a massive spring tide. It is then possible to see Park Gate as it was all those years ago, with the high tide lipping the sandstone of the embankment walls. The cottages are still there, of course, as is the customs house and the slipways.

All that is missing are the shallow-drafted, two-masted packet boats, waiting for the tide to cast off for their next trip to Dublin …

'Tell me sir, is yer bound, loik me, fer Dublin on the next packet?' says the stranger, looking up to a well-dressed man in his late twenties.

'Yes indeed,' he replies.

'Yer not to be returning home then, so?' says the stranger.

'No, sir,' he replies. 'I have to arrange new imports of cowhides and calfskins and other items for my family's business. We make shoes, you see. Our Irish supplier has sent a letter with new prices and I need to renegotiate or find other means. We have a neighbour who has asked me look into importing good linen too.'

'Is that so, sir? Well, me name is Hugh, and we know Park Gate well. Me and my missus here, Beth, are in good shape but getting on now. Thank the lord we return each summer, as autumn creeps on, to make hay and reap corn at an estate near Wolver'ampton. It's hard work but the mester pays good, and we sleep, with several other harvesters, in a dry, comfortable banrach. The mester's even built a common privy, so he has, and there's clean running water. We've been coming to his farm these past six years. We are simple culchies sir; without this work we cannot afford our rent back home: a single-bedroom cottage, sir, in County Kildare, with a few head of cattle. It's taken us five days of hard walking to get here from the farm near Wolver'ampton. But we were well met on the road. Kind folk offered us dry shelter and a comfortable place to sleep. We know this way well. Like the back of me hand. How's about you'se, sir?'

'My family resides near Lichfield,' says the young man. 'We make all manner of shoes and boots. This is my first trip. I took the chaise to Chester. It's costly, and I was unaware of a few hidden items, so I walked the last 8 miles to get here. I travel light with just one bag. Please call me Thomas, Thomas Hardman, at your service.'

'Hugh O'Connor, sir. Your first time, eh? You'll do well to take good care here in Park Gate. The few innkeepers have demand in full, and don't they know it. But many returning labourers, like us, prefer Park Gate to the Head [Holyhead]. The road to Anglesey is a rough old tramp through mountains, taking ten days or more. Better to wait here on the gentle Dee; locals call it Chester Water. In days gone you could leave Chester by packet to the old country, but now silt plays havoc, so it does. Even though they've cut a new channel, these packets do not have the shallow draught to clear to Chester unless on a full moon tide. For sure, Park Gate do mean a longer sea journey. In fact, twice as long, they say.'

'Tell me, Hugh, do you know when the Queen is to leave?'

'Sir, I wish I knew. I've heard tell that a captain will wait till his vessel has a full passenger quota before he weighs anchor. It is not helped that we sail against prevailing westerlies. Them Welsh hills *across the estuary there play havoc with the wind. A fair wind, if you please, and a good tide on the ebb. On all our six returns to Dublin, we failed to leave on time, so we did. Delays can be up to a week, but my guess is a couple of days. If I may be bold, sir – best advice and the first rule – only embark when the captain embarks.'*

'That's interesting,' says Thomas. 'When I was planning this trip, I was told the Head is more reliable as departing is easier, but it means extra and difficult travelling through North Wales and Anglesey, which all adds to the cost. I have to be careful with my expenses.'

'Ah, they're stories put about by the mail packet companies at the Head, so they are,' replies Hugh. 'They say Park Gate is unreliable, but methinks they play up these delays to their own advantage. They also tell of short crossing times from the Head to Dublin. They claim a best time of ten hours, but I hear that a fast time is more like twenty. No, sir, Park Gate is fine … well, fine, I guess, till Liverpool's packet boats become more regular. To be sure, Liverpool will soon be the port for Dublin, and it won't be long, let me tell you. Isn't that the truth of it, now?'

'Thank you, Hugh. I'll keep tabs on the departure of the next packet. I can see two fine vessels tied up along the quay. The larger, three-master, is the packet I've booked, Queen. What do you know of the second vessel, a rather splendid-looking boat with two masts?'

'Ah sir, that's Dorset. I happen to know an Irish lad who was press-ganged into the Navy in Liverpool and put aboard Dorset. She belongs to His Majesty – part of the Royal Navy she is – and is there at His Majesty's instruct. She's on government business in Ireland, based at the Dublin station. She travels often to Waterford, Belfast and Holyhead, sometimes down to Portsmouth for repair. So my pal says. She takes passengers on government business, but she do take private bookings if they have space. I hear tell that she is pricey but has all manner of luxury. But that's as much as I know, sir.'

'Oh, I see,' says Thomas, 'She looks a fine vessel and I guess she's ideally suited to these shallow waters. Do you have any appointments, Hugh? As I don't want to keep you from them.'

'What me? No, none, sir. Me and Beth fancy a stroll along this parade in the afternoon's warmth. We'll then take a walk on the strand, beyond Boathouse Hole. But there's a great view of the estuary if we walk south to where the promenade starts. Then it's a short walk uphill to higher ground, the promontory not that far from Neston. We went there last year. You have a fine view of all the traffic on the Dee. I'm told this was once a camp for Norse settlers from my own Dublin, back in the day.'

'If I may indulge your patience further,' says Thomas, 'I will do as you bid to take care in these parts, but a few minutes ago you mentioned a first rule, "only embark when the captain embarks". What be the other rules?'

'Ah them rules, sir. Yes, two more as I recall, given to us by a travelling preacher man by the name of Wesley, two years back, when he was waiting for his packet to Dublin. His second was "only pay the mester when you actually sail", and the third, sir, "never send your luggage to a vessel in advance"; do always take whatever luggage you have with you.'

'Thank you once again, Hugh; you have given me a little confidence. You see, I'm here at the behest of my father, and I carry heavy responsibilities for the family shoemaking business. I have to say I'm a little frightened by this passage. I've never been to sea before. My father was not keen for me to go, you see – he thought I needed a few more years – but there you are.'

'I'm sure you will do well for your owl fella, but if I may, sir, we have a wee saying where I'm from: "You've got to do your own growing, no matter how tall yer father was." I'm sure you'll grow nicely into your father's shoes. Now, Mester Thomas, when you're out at sea and you feel unwell due to the motion of the boat, then you stays on deck as long as you can and keep looking into the far distance. You may well be fine, young feller, some folk travel well first time. Others take to their bunk, if they have one.'

'Thank you, Hugh, and one more thing if you have time. I was told at my overnight lodgings to beware of the correction house at the Old Quay.'

'Do you see that red brick building along the quay, some 100 yards upriver from here? That's the correction house. I am told it has over 30 Irish folks, some with their young 'uns, all waiting for that fair wind to take 'em home. Until time for departure, they're put to hard labour. The local gentry, here in Park Gate, call those poor wretches "convicted rogues and vagabonds". That is mightily unfair, so it is. They've hit hard times, having to beg for bread and buttermilk, and sleep rough with no work. They come over to find work as labourers, struggle, and before long seek alms. Brought before the beak for begging in the street, it's their lot to be served a warrant of expulsion to be sent back to their place of legal settlement. Back to Ireland simply because they were begging for food. Bless 'em, they do no wrong. Like me and Beth here, they made the crossing some weeks ago. The only wrong done 'em was to find no work during harvest.

'I will say also this, sir,' he went on. 'You English folk do look after 'em. They're fed and their health is checked in the poorhouse. If they were in Ireland, suffering the same distress, they'd be left alone to fend for theirselves.'

'Thank you again, Hugh, for your advice. I will take care. Do you think those folks will be on my packet?'

'Indeed, they will, sir, but it is unlikely yer will meet up, so. They're the first to be loaded because their house on the quay needs the space for yet more "vagabonds". They'll be held below decks in the cargo hold, and bought on deck only in an emergency.

'Those in the Old Quay House of Correction are not to worry yer good self,' he continued. 'But come here to me now; there are other dangers, especially for newcomers. Pickpockets work this promenade and port, so they do. We sew our valuables and cash into our clothes. Without cash, yer doomed, sir. There is no ready credit for us travellers, whatever their place.'

'I will take my leave of you, Hugh, Beth. Thank you kindly for your help. I feel a little better about facing the passage. I hope to see you on board. Good day to you both, and thank you once again.'

Hugh thinks of his passage home with Beth, and how in a few days from now they will arrive in Dublin Quay or Dún

Laoghaire, whichever the captain chooses as right. They will then have another three-day walk out to their cottage in Kildare – but happily now, with money to pay the winter's rent.

Thomas shakes hands with them and starts to take off on a slow stroll along the sea front towards the packet company's berthed three-mast brig, but not before one final question: 'Good advice, and thank you, Hugh. But if I may finally ask: why do you both carry your shoes around your neck?'

'Simple, sir. We need to be careful with our monies. Why wear 'em out when we're not harvesting or on a hard slog on rough ground?'

13

AFON ALYN

It comes as little surprise that North Wales is to be our next adventure. Those Welsh hills have been a constant draw in our travels along Wirral's coastline. We want to climb Moel Ffamau, the western mountain we see from the marshes near Parkgate, with its fascinating, nipple-like squat tower. It was Roy who had pointed this out this when we left Parkgate. I had looked back and smirked ever so slightly.

Timetable research confirms there's another Crosville bus, this time the F1, also from Birkenhead's Woodside terminus, which will take us to a place called Loggerheads. It's an hour's journey and, reading our Ordnance Survey map, we see that from there it will be a good two-hour hike to the top of Moel Ffamau. Providing we get the first bus we will have time enough to climb the mountain and get the last bus back. We decide on a Saturday trip in mid-May.

When the dark green Crosville is 20 minutes out of Birkenhead it takes a right at a major junction and descends towards the Dee Estuary. The boundary with Wales at this point is the River Dee, but little changes in the scenery as our route crosses the muddy and slow river near Holywell. We pass the Welcome to Wales sign.[37]

---

37 'In the 1960s, the Welsh Language Society (Cymdeithas yr Iaith Gymraeg) decided to instigate a campaign to deface and remove English-only road signs in order to force local authorities and government to install bilingual signs. The campaign, a source of disquiet at the time due to its simplicity and visibility, was ultimately successful and led to bilingual road signs throughout Wales.' BBC *On the Brink*, 2008. Of late, all new road signs have the Welsh version first, but this was not always the case. Thankfully we now have 'Croeso y Cymru' to replace 'Welcome to Wales'.

The road winds up through villages of neat terraced cottages built out of locally quarried, charcoal-grey limestone. Green fields spread across rising lowlands until the old coach road from Chester arrives at the wide streets of the market town of Mold,[38] our penultimate stop. It's not quite 8 o'clock in the morning.

Our bus waits a few minutes with the engine running. The driver must be slightly ahead of schedule. From upstairs we see a slow, snail-slow, early morning tempo. A deliberate orderliness to the day's beginnings. Mold will not be rushed. A few shops have unwound their red and white striped awnings, and fresh milk bottles stand sentry on polished red steps. Early pedestrians potter and chat. A grocer in his olive-green pinafore carefully assembles his pavement display: oranges, tangerines, lemons and limes, Maris Pipers and King Edwards, cauliflower and kale. He interrupts his creation to serve a tall lady in a smart grey slimline coat and matching shoes. She is pushing a navy-blue Silver Cross pram and stops and points to some greens. He picks a few runner beans. Proudly, she lets him peek at her new snuggled-up babe. There's no rush, and there is certainly time for gentle gossip in this settled market town.

Farmers in their battle-green land rovers pulling empty cattle carts wait patiently at traffic lights. A farmhand in his working blues and a duffel coat passes near to the bus, his head down, pulling on the lead of his reluctant black and white dog. He turns the corner and is gone.

Over the road a young lad of nine or ten returns on his bike to the newsagent, his canvas bag empty of its *Mirrors* and *Mails*. Mold is slowly getting into its Saturday stride as we pull away and head west for the near hills.

Our ride finishes at Loggerheads, a short ten-minute journey from Mold, just inside the county of Denbighshire. A small village with a pub, a garage with two petrol pumps, an old, disused flour mill and a few stone cottages. Its clumsy English name sits oddly alongside the nearby villages of Pantymwyn and Gwernymynydd. It is thought to derive from a dispute over the estate boundaries between the lordships of Mold and Llanferres.[39]

---

38 The name does not mean what you might think; it derives from the Norman French '*mont hault*', high hill. (*Oxford Names Companion*, 2002)

39 The very word 'loggerheads' derives from a bitter mining dispute of this time. You can still see a plaque above the boundary stone on the A494 erected following the resolution of a quarrel between the supremely rich and powerful Grosvenor family, who owned the mineral rights in the parish of Llanferres, and the Lords of Mold, who owned those in Mold parish and eventually won.

The bus finally pulls into its nondescript terminus, a patch of waste ground covered in black cinder holding fresh rainwater puddles. A green bus stop sign is hidden amongst overgrown bushes alongside a footpath sign which points the way to the river. A strange place, with old buildings in need of repair and affection. All is muted and deserted as nature feels its way back. A friendly beech tree sits alongside a roofless stone ruin, once the flour mill. Thirty feet of smooth, silvery trunk reaching up. Its roots disturb the old, misshapen mill wall. Overhead the canopy is dense and little light gets through. Shiny leaves of soft green spread their cover and shade. Underfoot layers of crisp brown discarded and now dried leaves crunch to the tread. Old beechmast, ideal squirrel fodder but now bereft of its scrunchy seeds, lies in scattered leaf litter.

The space where a waterwheel once churned is empty, covered in nettles and beech saplings.[40] Ragwort and thistles cling to old limestone walls as nature takes back what was always hers.

A stout wooden bridge crosses the River Alyn[41] into a new world. Over many millennia the Alyn, a tributary of the River Dee, has cut through local porous limestone to form a gorge 3 miles long and in places 100 feet deep. There are stretches of dry riverbed where the river finds a path underground; another world, cutting through the centuries-soluble limestone. Our footpath takes us on an open one-mile stretch. To the right are several head-high cavities of sliding fractures in the limestone. A few bats fly out and one catches in Roy's hair. We slowly remove it. Roy thinks it's a common pipistrelle.

Old local sinkholes are fenced off, and grassy banks form over debris left from long gone, open-cast lead mines. This valley carries its Roman past gently, almost surreptitiously, to its bosom. Should we be intruding? We mean no harm.

Soft morning light, filtered by a leafy canopy, dapples on groundcover of green garlic, highlighting their petite, spiky white florets. Ash is

---

40   This used to house a 40-foot-diameter water wheel. Water was used to power several mills on the River Alyn, including the Pentre Mill which dates from at least the late 18th century. The mill originally ground corn but became a sawmill in the late 19th century. A dynamo was added in the 1920s to generate electricity for local homes.

41   Around England and Wales there are many rivers called Allan, Alyn, Allen, Alun; this indicates that the word means 'river' and is of ancient origin – Celtic, or even earlier.

dominant along this karstic cut. Two mature trees sit either side of the path. Each reaches up to the sky, erect and pushy. Mature ash has a beige-tinted bark, smooth compared to that of a gnarled old oak. Ash branches cascade down, almost touching the path. Oval leaves sway gently in their symmetry, pairs forming at regular intervals along this year's new growth, leaving enough light for smooth-trunked saplings in their fresh lime-green livery to try their luck.

The diffuse cover of these two ashes also supports a few coppiced hazel shrubs, a sign of old woodland knowledge on this stretch of the Alyn. These bushes have been coppiced just above ground level. The result is a thick bush made of many narrow independent trunks, producing stiff, sprouting hazel, ideal for walking sticks or in earlier times the wattle in wattle and daub.

Mixed stands of silver birch, elm and beech offer softer and harder greens. The odd willow, and occasional oak, are found along the path upstream. The broad river here is only a foot deep; fast clear water cascades over moss-free, smooth, glistening river boulders.

Mac tugs at my sleeve. 'There, over there,' he whispers and points.

A dipper stands on a cobble in the middle of the stream where the water is 6 inches deep, bobbing and curtseying to an imaginary royal. Russet underparts, white bib, brown uppers. Bright, dark eyes. No bigger than a small, dumpy thrush. We think female, but we really have no idea, just another intuitive guess. Hidden biases at play, or a sixth sense? Insight? Perhaps.

She dips deeper into the cold bright spate. Heavy, she treads the river's bed. Air bubbles trapped in her feathers shine like tiny drops of quicksilver. She presses on, head-first, hard against the river's pressure wave. She swims with the current, back to her cherished cobble. Shakes off the water and curtseys. Her stout beak is full of the cold stream's harvest, laden with larvae. She blinks and shows a third, ghostly, white eyelid to the world.

She cocks her head to one side, looks up to the trees. Two more instinctive curtseys. The dipper is off upstream, carrying a caddis fly larva shell, her wings whirring to a blur. She's gone. A vivid memory. (*Photo 28*)

A bird of wonder, the dipper, also known as a water ouzel. A passerine, no bigger than a song thrush, that walks and feeds underwater in fast-flowing streams full of invertebrate life. Our dipper has evolved a fine toolkit for its aquatic life.[42]

The white eyelid is new to us. We later find out it's called a nictitating membrane, a third eyelid which operates laterally, not vertically. It's found in many fish, reptiles, birds and mammals – but, surprisingly not in primates.[43] In many underwater species, the membrane is translucent, a protective device which does not hinder sight. In the species which also spend time out of the water, the membrane blinks involuntarily (the Latin for 'blink' is *nectare*) helping to remove any dirt or dust particles and keeping the eye moist.

Roy looks carefully for one of his target species and finds them, a swathe of purple common spotted orchids in grasses on the side of our path, no bigger than 6 inches at their tallest. Orchids carry in their name the exotica of elsewhere, but here they grow charmingly alongside pungent wild garlic, bluebells, white wood anemones and yellow lesser celandines. Roy's appetite is whetted; we are all on the lookout for other orchid species.

The woodland canopy is not too dense in spring; easier to spot many male summer migrants declaring their territories in full voice, looking for mates. Males want to be seen as well as heard, so they find a conspicuous spot, often higher up on an exposed branch. A common redstart obliges on the other side of the river. A beautiful small bird, robin-sized with a glistening white forehead, silver crown, black cheeks and throat, and an orangey-red chest, upper belly and tail feathers. A colourful bird, its slate-grey wings add a reflective dash of local limestone.

---

42   Dippers are the only passerines able to swim and feed under water. Evolution has handed down specific adaptations to a life in water. Short and strong wings offer them a flipper-like action under water. Unlike other passerines, their bones are solid, not hollow, making them denser than water, which allows them to actually *walk* along the riverbed. Their preen glands are large for their size, to fully waterproof their dense feathers. They have evolved underwater vision by using stronger eye muscles to change the curvature of their lenses to manage refraction. They also have nasal flaps which act like one-way valves to prevent water entering their nostrils.

43   As a nine-year-old I had an irritating itch in my right eye and Dad suggested we visit the doctor. The doctor confirmed a shared diagnosis at my birth: I had a misshapen right eyeball, thought to be a leftover from the third eyelid present in many mammals. I had an overnight stay at St Paul's Eye Hospital in Liverpool, and an operation to remove the offending tissue. We had left home in Leasowe with a bag for my nightclothes, and I have never forgotten that when we were catching the ferry over to Liverpool my Dad asked for one adult return and one child single. Scary stuff!

Shady ash provides ideal refuge for spotted flycatchers, sparrow-sized migrants from sub-Saharan Africa, mostly brown above and creamy-white beneath but with a streaked breast and cap. One of these birds regularly lifts off from its favourite perch, catches a nearby flying insect and returns to the same shaded perch to feast. There's a clue in its name. We watch this behaviour for a good 15 minutes until the local invertebrate larder is empty. It then moves off to another preferred shady patch under the ash to look again for insect life. This bird has just arrived from its mammoth migration, so it needs to build up weight quickly before mating starts, probably in a couple of days. (*Photo 29*)

An hour into this foreign patch, almost a foreign country, and so much new fauna and flora. Roy puts it all down to limestone geography. Slowly it dawns on us; we are on one of nature's unintended adrenaline rushes. We knew when we set off from Woodside that this could well be one of those days. Can it get any better? What will the rest of the day bring?

The map shows a bridge upstream carrying a track where we need to cross back over the river. There are more remnants of bygone industry, overgrown and hidden by resurgent nature. Nearby is evidence of the leat, a man-made channel which once carried water to local lead mines. We leave the Alyn gorge when our footpath crosses the bridge, and the track climbs gently to the fields at the foot of Moel Famau.

A change in light intensity or wind direction wants to surprise and challenge. Today's cold, sharp northerlies offer dryness and austerity to complement nature's soft tones. Strong sunlight after a recent sharp shower on a heather moor above us lifts out hidden heather magentas, olive-green silver birch saplings and bright oilskin-yellow flowering broom.

Hedged fields here at the foot of the Clwyddian Hills slope up into small U-shaped valleys. We hear a sharp trill echoing from the hillside, followed by a soft, chattering burble. A new bird call? We keep to the hedgerows for cover, for fear of trespass still. In a far corner, high in a hawthorn, sits a large, dark thrush. It has the appearance of a male blackbird with its yellow beak – but surely a blackbird would be smaller. A mewing call from the skies above echoes off the hillside as a soaring buzzard notes our slow, clumsy progress. The ground underfoot is boggy and uneven; ideal for local sheep and rabbits, but heavy and difficult for young humans. As we get close, the black bird sees us and turns on his perch, proudly displaying a white crescent of chest feathers against the rest of his chest of dark brown scallop shapes with light grey trims.

A fine singing male ring ouzel, probably nesting. This is heaven! We sit and watch for several minutes as the bird flies down to the ground searching for grubs and then returns to his favourite perch, high in the hawthorn. Our own Elysian Field. We sit down, take stock and make more notes. First a water ouzel, now a ring ouzel.

After the excitement ebbs, we worry over our timetable. We need to get back to our original path, which will take us up Moel Ffamau. It's only 1,600 feet high, but in our book it's a mountain.

We retrace our path, over a wooden stile, and are soon back on the long ascent which leads directly up the mountain. This is not an easy, contour-hugging trail. It's a tough, steep climb through young conifers planted by the Forestry Commission. A quick look back. There's Loggerheads, hidden in trees by the main road, and in the far distance we see for the first time the full extent of the Dee Estuary. There's Hilbre. There's the Cheshire plain. There's the Wirral Peninsula.

Just another 150 feet to climb. The gradient is shallower now and as the top of our mountain comes into view we see the tower appear. What from a distance was a squat shape on top of a distant hill is a rubble-strewn, part-demolished tower, approximate 20 yards square.[44]

We climb the summit, and the westerly hits hard. It's difficult to stand as the wind shears off the top of the ruin. Ravens cronk to each other across the hillsides as a kestrel hovers close, below us. Rain droplets on its waterproof brown back glint in the pale clear light. The kestrel's head is completely still, whilst its neck and body, tail and wings adjust to the tricky wind conditions. Meadow pipits 'tseep' in lavender-coloured heather.

Looking east from this higher ground, we see the distant, mighty Anglican cathedral of Liverpool. There's the Mersey, a thin sliver of light reflections. Our world of Birkenhead and Wallasey, once our entire world, is reduced to a tiny segment of the 180-degree vista.

---

44   The building was started in 1810 to celebrate the golden jubilee of King George III. Its original design was of an obelisk, but it was never finished. In 1860 a severe storm damaged the construction, and for safety reasons it was reduced to the single storey which survives. Since then, unused stone has been removed, and much of it used to repair nearby dry-stone walls.

It dawns on us we have crossed a significant border, not simply the divide between England and Wales. Beneath us is a summary of the world before today. Hilbre looks so small. We make out Burton Marshes next to the steelworks. That must be Parkgate, where a row of minuscule buildings confronts the marsh. Where's Leasowe?

In later life I read the Arthurian tales. I wonder, now, if the view of the Wirral wilderness from the summit of Moel Ffamau was that seen by Sir Gawain when he searched for a rematch with the Green Knight, torn as he was between truth and his chivalric loyalties to his lord. His search is thought to have taken him to the Wirral, via a ford across the River Dee near Holywell.[45]

The wind blows hard, and a quick look over our shoulders; west again. More mountains. Proper mountains this time. Snowdon is the highest peak, at more than twice our current elevation.

We have two and a half hours to make tracks back to Loggerheads for the last bus. There's time for a quick detour as we hear a nearby cuckoo. A natural bowl in the lower moor holds a hawthorn copse and plenty of gorse. A male cuckoo has chosen this sheltered dell to declare his desires. He sits proudly on a dead but stout hawthorn stump calling to the world. His long, fanned tail feathers anchor his balance in the fresh wind.

Our path takes us back along the Afon Alyn, the friend we made earlier in the day, the river which has been running its course for millennia, saluting those who mined the lead, cut the leat, coppiced the hazel and lived their lives. Our water ouzel is still dipping and bobbing. The friendly beech by the old mill provides a final shelter from a short shower. The day is done.

Our knowledge of nature, like a fine block of hardened ash, is slowly being honed and carved into shape. Surfaces are being rubbed down to a smooth shell. Experience is the sculptor, nature's wonder is the piece of art.

The Alyn of our youth had that illusive, ephemeral magic offering fleeting glimpses of nature's beauty, like the wondrous ghostly traces left by

---

45   For a modern version of *Sir Gawain and the Green Knight* do try Simon Armitage's work, published in 2008.

decaying sub-atomic particles after a high-energy particle collision in a bubble chamber. Momentary traces of a hidden world now lost in time.

This year, walking down the river has brought back memories of the two ouzels and the limestone-loving orchids. But unlike a few places I have revisited after a long absence, Loggerheads seems to have suffered most. A busy and beneficial nature park with its obligatory café and toilets. Busy with many families and their dogs enjoying the trees and the river. As young teenagers we had the place to ourselves. We felt we had discovered it, when clearly we had done no such thing.

Those were formative ages, 13 and 14. We visited the Alyn in its various seasonal guises. So perhaps it's a mistake to go back all those years later. Do we break adolescent spells, never intended to be fractured, when we return to favourite haunts? Were we excessively entranced and enchanted by the new world of limestone geography and zoology? New botany, new birds, new worlds.

Loggerheads had something else to add to nature's brew. Remnants, generational ghosts of old technology, when the Alyn's waters were diverted to the leat to power a large watermill to grind corn. Hidden now by nature's green shroud; grassy uneven contours of unwanted topsoil waste, sunken pits from the days of open cast mining.

When we boys crossed the River Dee[46] we crossed the Welsh border, naïvely expecting nature to be different simply because here was a new country. But the contrasts were not there. A few Welsh place names, an occasional overheard Welsh conversation, but that was it. Human constructs. The natural world does not do white-lines-on-the-ground boundaries, clearly defined edges, to help humans navigate nature's imagined peripheries.

Nature's subtle changes are often unseen to the casual eye. Follow a stream to its source: you must look carefully to see those hairline changes in grasses, plants and shrubs. These variations dictated by *terroir*. In wine-speak, terroir is not just the soil condition but includes other influences such as local temperature variations, natural wind directions, whether the land is south or north-facing and so on. In fact, terroir is best translated as the interaction between microclimate and geography,

---

46   In the British Isles there are five rivers called Dee, and that name too is an early, probably Celtic, one; it means 'goddess, holy place'.

including the make-up of the soil. Walk up a mountain track; at a certain height a hedgerow slowly thins until an undefined line is reached where small trees do not grow. They simply can't survive. Turn a corner along a lush lane into a north-facing terrace, and vegetation can be scarce. Nature's boundaries are liminal.

Man-made boundaries on the other hand are defined by differences of language and culture. Man-made boundaries are willed politically or forced militarily; agreed between groups or imposed by one group on another. A few political boundaries are arbitrary straight lines on a map, extending the horror days of empire and colonialism.

As far as we know, birds have no such social or cultural conventions. Let's take one example of a cultural construct involving boundaries, the idea of a home. If it were possible to ask a cuckoo where 'home' is she would most probably reply,

> *I'm not sure what you mean by home. I spend most of my time in a large area of the tropics (West Africa), apart from three or four months when I fly north or north-east cross a vast arid desert (Sahara) or sea (Indian Ocean). If I go over the Sahara there is then a large sea (Mediterranean) to cross. Eventually I end up in a Scottish glen near where I was born. When I arrive in Scotland the days are longer than in Africa and suitable food is normally abundant. There is, therefore, more time to find a mate, lay 15 or so eggs, all in different nests of the species which fostered me. My own foster parents were reed warblers. As soon as I have laid the last egg, I'm done. I quickly feed up and find my way back to the tropics, and let new foster parents do all the work to feed the youngsters who I will never see. I may not make it back to West Africa. I'm only away for three, possibly, four, months at most.*[47]

So, if the definition of home is where we spend most of our lives, for the cuckoo it's equatorial West Africa. If the definition of home is where we are born, it's Scotland. The point here of course is that we are applying a cultural idea to a bird which does not have that concept. Our cuckoo

---

47   For more information, *Cuckoo, Cheating by Nature* by Nick Davies, published in 2015, offers a rare glimpse of an evolutionary arms race between cuckoos and their hosts. Nick Davies is both a naturalist and a scientist, and he leads the reader through the escalating deceptions played by the cuckoo on the host and the hosts' equally escalatory retaliatory strategies.

has instinct, incredible navigational skills and the wherewithal to survive enormous journeys, but when we posit such ideas as a cuckoo's home and boundaries we are being anthropomorphic.

Arctic terns breed in or near the Arctic Circle and migrate in September to the Antarctic: from one pole to the other, over 19,000 kilometres. They then return to the Arctic in the spring of the northern hemisphere. So these birds never experience long winter nights. Twelve hours of darkness at most, and that only for a few days when they cross the equator twice a year.

More detailed research, from the Netherlands, has recently shown the routes taken by Arctic terns suggest that their round-trip distance is more like 90,000 kilometres. Ringing records have shown that these birds can live up to 30 years. A quick tot-up makes that a possible distance of 2,700,000 kilometres in a lifetime, equivalent to flying to the moon and back three and a half times. The Arctic tern and many other terns follow a migratory pattern. They have no boundaries as such. The planet itself is their territory or 'home'.

On a personal level, I don't get the fuss over boundaries. My own cultural background, or baggage, happens to be one of a woolly-back scouser, a northerner. I'm happy with that and have been known to welcome the stereotype, using the odd joke about southern softies, especially at football games.

I am aware, though, that my cultural heritage is an accident of birth. I like to think that this recognition is important. We belong to the planet, just like the Arctic tern.

14

PINKFEET

It's late October. First frosts bite hard. The alarm clock is set for 6 a.m. Bedsheets are warm and cosy. Behind the lace curtains, condensation bedews the cold glass pane. Why did I agree to go on this trip? Why, oh why? If the alarm did not wake up our kid, then switching on the bedroom light does. I'm determined to go on this school natural history outing for a reason which right now I can't quite fathom. In the cold, speed is essential. Dressed in a minute and down to the equally cold kitchen to collect sandwiches and drinks, which Mum prepared last night.

'Not cheese and pickle again, Ma!'

Streetlamps shine their pale orange-yellow sodium glow on damp pavements. It's a five-minute walk to the bus stop, then two buses to get to the rendezvous. The final bus crosses the Penny Bridge over the docks to Birkenhead as a pink dawn breaks slowly. The waterfront is crammed with ships, but these vessels are lifeless, frozen in time with their skeletal string-set of bulbs offering patterned pinpoints of intense candlepower.

Our group is six; seven when you include our leader, an older lad by the name of Colin. The rest of us are 13 and 14-year-olds in our wellies, anoraks and rucksacks. Colin has the map. He's taking us to the flat stubble fields of west Lancashire, near Burscough, in search of two species of winter visitors from the Arctic. When we finally arrive at Crossens station, it's a dull, overcast morning. We take stock. Final adjustments to rucksacks, binoculars at the ready, we look for the Way Out sign and show our tickets to the inspector. The level crossing gates open and we follow Colin's directions, taking a right along a lane for a mile.

After 20 minutes we hear strange, disorienting, dim nasal calls coming from the distant western horizon, the darkest part of the sky. The noise grows until Colin points and says, '*There they are!*'

Our binoculars pick up V-shaped lines of geese, followed by yet more chevrons. The excited, high-pitched 'oinks' get louder still. The boisterous nasal sound has echoes of wilderness, of enchantment, of mystery.

No-one speaks. We stand and stare in wonder at this amazing spectacle. These are wild grey geese. This is migration at first hand. Strings of birds continue overhead in their thousands for a good ten minutes, filling the low western horizon with their long-line patterns. We witness one of nature's jaw-dropping raw scenes. The outriders leading this dark grey silhouetted blizzard of geese start to descend. The scouts must know there are many more behind, so wherever they choose must be right. They decide on a particularly large field of dark brown, almost black, soil flecked with neat lines of straw-yellow potato stubble. This is the signal for the trailing birds to follow suit. It takes a good ten minutes for the entire flock to descend, layer after layer, slowly disappearing into early morning's grey shadows. (*Photo 30*)

At just 500 feet or so above ground, some individual geese show off their avian acrobatics with a sudden tumble, dropping 20 feet or more as if they have hit an air pocket. This is whiffling, a unique way of achieving a very quick descent. When flying, a goose can turn its body upside down whilst not moving its head from its normal position. So whatever aerodynamics are used to get lift, the same aerodynamics are reversed, and descent is an instantaneous controlled fall.

'These are all pink-footed geese,' Colin says, 'arriving from Iceland, and a few from eastern Greenland.'

'How did he know the Greenland bit?' I thought to myself.

He continues in his inimitable matter-of-fact way. 'Pinkfeet are a tad smaller than our resident greylag, and more timid. Darker heads, a small pink bill with a black tip – and yes, pink feet. This huge flock may have come directly from Iceland, but more likely from their stopover in a few selected locations in Scotland, especially the Firths of Moray and Solway, probably Solway.'

These geese are feeding on stubble left over from harvested summer crops of maize, sugar beet and potatoes. Our aim is to get close to these surprisingly timid Arctic wanderers. It's not going to be easy. They have landed a good mile away, so we stick to our original track, which heads in that direction. But our gravel path soon curves away from our target area, so we take a narrow track along the edge of a field where there's a meagre, windblown hawthorn hedge offering cover of sorts. We all know to keep *shtum*. Young hunters armed only with a notebook and a pair of field glasses.

The gaunt hedgerow stops abruptly at the corner of the field. Morning's light has arrived; we are clearly visible to an alert wild goose. What now? If we want to get close, it has to be the adjacent damp ditch. We scramble down the grassy bank, keeping our heads low. We walk on carefully for another 100 yards. Colin leads, we follow. He's taller than us, and can just see over the bank we are following. Suddenly he stops and points to a spot above the bank, his other hand with a straight forefinger over his sealed lips.

We crawl up the bank trying not to break cover, lie on damp grass and absorb the image. There in front of us are thousands of wild geese who have just flown the 800 miles from their breeding grounds in Iceland, maybe directly. Their non-stop flight to Scotland alone lasts 20 hours, less with a favourable tailwind. This one field must contain at least 1,000 hungry birds. On the menu today are yellow stalks left by the harvester, the few remaining green shoots and spare spuds the harvester missed. The nearest group, 30 yards away, is 14 in number. A few extended families. One bird is on lookout duty, head held high, sniffing the air. The rest feed. Distant social oink calls from the flock provide a garrulous motif carried to us by the light breeze.

Left alone they will feed here all day, returning to the marshy mudflats on the coast to roost, to sleep safe from disturbance. The pinkfeet wanderers are ever watchful. Alert yet tired, aware of danger, but hungry, needing to feed.

The commotion starts in the far corner. A group of pinkfeet sounds the alarm and takes to vertical flight. Soon the entire flock takes off in one long rising, rippling wave. The sudden uproar is deafening; a cacophony of pinkfeet. Geese in other fields follow suit. What has caused this mass uprising? Was it us? We look at each other, but we don't think it was us, given the eruption started in a far corner. Maybe a tractor, maybe a walker with a loose dog. After several noisy minutes the geese find another nearby location, descend and dine. The field which was a busy feeding ground is once again cold, scrubbed stubble.

We sit on the bank and share the moment. It's late morning, dry and cold but not icy. It's time to open our rucksacks and tuck into our packed lunches even though it's not quite midday. A nibble of a sandwich, a bite of biscuit and sips of warm coffee from the thermos whilst Colin explains how these wild geese share the work of flying.

'The chevron-shaped flying formation works to the flock's advantage,' he says. 'Each trailing bird on either side of the leader gets help from the bird in front, each one behind meeting with less wind resistance. The onerous job of being a lead bird is shared. Watch them next time, and you'll see this role rotated amongst all in the chevron.' (*Photo 31*)

Colin tells us these birds are here for the winter before leaving around April, when they will travel north back to the land of their birth just in time for the first touch of Arctic spring.

These wild geese are huge flocks of feeding birds. But unknown to our casual glimpse, they are made of family groups who stay together for the winter. They are safer feeding in groups than on their own; more eyes to detect danger.

Theirs is a collective life. An idea which I find appealing. Six young lads exploring nature in our own tight group. To repeat my earlier point, in birdwatching terms six pairs of eyes are always better than one, just as it is for the birds themselves.

We are in a comparatively unknown area, Martin Mere, enjoying our early lunch in what was once the largest lake in England, albeit quite shallow, formed when water filled a huge depression left by retreating glaciers. Borrowing on the work going on in the Lincolnshire fens at the time, attempts to drain the large mere by wind power were started in the early 1700s, to provide fertile agricultural land.

The lake was eventually drained completely when efficient steam engines took over from the windmills in the mid-19th century. We pass one of those disused windmills. Painted white, with its four sails long gone. All that remains are the four massive timbers reaching out to garner those westerlies. She sits proudly at the intersection of two drainage channels, her work done.

It's midday, time for our second quest. Colin suggests we head eastwards towards Mere Brow: 'When I was last there I found a group of wintering wild swans who also had a taste for potatoes.' He consults his map and reckons, 'It's a 30-minute walk on flat, easy tracks.'

We pass neat stacks of large, empty wooden crates and disturb a small goldfinch flock as they scrabble for seeds in dried thistle heads. Further along the lane flighty linnets pick over discarded grain seeds along the dirt track. A lumbering grey heron rises slowly from the ditch ahead, calling out an ancient and threatening 'vraaak, vraaak' to our group. She passes back over our heads before taking up sentry duty behind us in the water's edge; motionless for minutes until she daggers her prey with her long, primitive spear of a beak.

More linnets take to a twittering flight. High overhead a bird is heard mewing, 'pee-yah, pee-yah'. The buzzard slowly circles upwards. Wide circles. Flap flap, glide, flap flap, glide.

After 20 minutes the track ahead rises slightly, and from this extra elevation of just a few feet we pick up in our binoculars a group of 20-plus swans on our right, most with their heads down, feeding. They have the build of our resident mute swans. But these are normally seen only in pairs or a small family group of three or four, so a group of this size suggests another species altogether. As we get close, the wind carries their occasional honking chatter.

Wild geese just after breakfast and wild swans just after lunch.

We creep closer until we can go no further. Wild swans from Iceland. Whooper swans. All white, apart from their black legs and black beaks. Although it's unusual in the bird world for us to see markings specific to individuals, the triangle of vivid yellow on the upper mandible of adult whoopers varies in shape from one adult bird to another, like a fingerprint only more visible. The group are feeding on potatoes which have been overlooked by the mechanical harvester, mainly at the pasture's perimeter. We count 23. Colin suggests there might be five or six family groups with at least one youngster each. The cygnets look to be this summer's offspring, their plumage a mixture of white and a mottled light sandy hue. These cygnets have not yet developed their yellow beak patches. Occasionally a couple of adult birds stand tall facing each other, indulging in aggressive wing-flapping whilst giving each other a noisy vocal ticking off. (*Photo 32*)

We are engrossed and watch these magnificent birds for a good half-hour before heading back along the track. We take a collective decision to return to Crossens. As we contemplate our early evening's journey back to Wallasey, the geese and swans think of their night time's roost. The geese will be out on the sea marsh and sandbanks off Southport. The swans will look for clear water.

Colin is poring over his Ordnance Survey map.

'I have an idea,' he says. 'There are a couple of ways we can make our way back to the station to get our train back to Liverpool. A short way and a long way. The long way, an extra 15 minutes, takes us alongside two drainage ditches. As we're getting to the end of the afternoon, we might see some owls.'

It's agreed. A little longer it is, and the possibility of an owl. Optimism again. We head off on a track on the perimeter of an old potato field, not disturbing the wild swans. The light is still reasonable, but the air is thin now. A chill has descended. The track does a left, and there ahead is a drainage ditch, 9 or 10 feet wide. The water is high, and our track accompanies the dyke for the next 2 miles. Colin stops.

'This is top hunting ground for owls, ideal vole country. These fields, either side of the canal, have laid fallow for a few years. As you can see, they're now overgrown with various plants and weeds, ideal for voles. You won't find many voles on those potato fields where the swans are. Owls also like to follow ditches as they hunt; more chance of spotting a vole or mouse.'

The group keep silent, our eyes peeled for owls. A few moorhen call out their 'krek-krek-krek' from depths of the bank's vegetation. A lone black-headed gull follows the wide ditch looking for food. We walk for a good 20 minutes before Colin mutters, 'Everybody down. There's a barn owl hunting along the far side of the ditch and it's coming our way. We need to be as quiet as possible. They have incredible hearing.'

We scramble down by the side of the ditch, using the bank's natural cover as much as possible. And wait. I can see it in the distance, coming towards us. The first impression is of an all-white bird, but when it gets near we can see light brown patterns on the flight feathers and back. The head is huge for its body. The slow flapping flight is eerily noiseless, not even a whisper. Silent stealth.

The wings beat slowly and deliberately as it wanders from one side of the ditch to the other, occasionally disappearing into the field but always coming back to the ditch. It hears something and hangs in the air. The white, slightly concave, facial disk acts as an amplifier for any animal noises. It hunts by listening for sounds in the undergrowth, hovers overhead and then dives head first from 4 feet or so and pounces with its white-feathered talons. We wait patiently to see if the bird emerges.

After a minute it rises from the undergrowth carrying a small mouse-like creature in one of its talons. It has caught something; it looks too big for a vole. 'Could be a mole,' says Colin. The owl carries it in one claw and flaps off across the field back to the ditch, exactly where we are sitting, and gives us a long stare. (*Photo 33*)

As the owl passes its stare is unbelievable, made more intense by the bright yellow irises and the way the head swivels to maintain the fix on us.

We look on intently as the bird flaps away from us.

'I wouldn't be surprised,' says Colin, 'if this bird is feeding a young brood, otherwise it would have stayed on the ground and fed there and then. Barn owls will time their breeding to match available food. At this time of the year this bird could well have a second brood. We've been lucky tonight to get so close. These apex predators, top of their food chain, are not found in large numbers.'

I try to listen carefully to what Colin has to say, but I daydream. I'm still in awe of this white owl. That stare, with its almost human face.

Return journeys offer the chance to collect thoughts. A loose group of young pilgrims on our furthest birding quest yet. Tracking down our wild wanderers. It's been a long day of adventure since the early alarm call under the warm sheets. By the time we get home our black books are full of scribbled notes and sketches, numbers and species.

We are birdwatchers. We chronicle. Three more ticks to add to the nitpickers' list. We call ourselves a natural history group. We have met before, but today's outing stretched us in many ways. We started off as a collection of individuals with a common interest, but the day's shared hikes, successes and chats has changed those dynamics. There's a shared joy in what we do. We end up a closer-knit group, prepared to help each other, look out for each other. That's a warm, decent feeling, well beyond the simple desire to belong.

The railway line from Liverpool which took us to Crossens station in the early 1960s sits to the north-west of what is now Martin Mere Wetlands, a nature reserve opened by the Wildfowl & Wetlands Trust in 1975. Some of the ditches and potato fields I tramped in the early sixties are part of this working reserve. My memory of those pinkfeet appearing out of the dawn skies above Martin Mere lives on.

Our collective human experiences with wild geese hints at a different world, appearing, as they tend to do, and as they did to me that day, out of the dawn. It is not surprising to find out that wild geese have a special part in many cultures.

There are several mythical tales of these wild travellers. Goose bones have been found in Neolithic excavations in Europe (around 10000–4000 BCE). Did those old bones carry a portentous, supernatural significance? There's a Celtic fable of geese travelling north to the mysterious lands of ice and snow to join up with a nether world. In Irish folklore, geese are described as having divine powers. Early Celtic Christians used wild geese rather than the dove as a metaphor to describe the holy spirit. At that time the holy spirit was understood to be quite capricious and not always a benevolent entity.

Another myth, this time from Germany, of Frau Holle, a goddess who lives deep in the mountain forest with her flock of geese. When she shakes her down-filled quilt, feathers fall as snow. Might this be a source of the fable of Mother Goose?

From Greece there are many images of Aphrodite, the goddess of love, riding a goose, and Hindu culture has a similar myth. Shakespeare delivered the phrase 'a wild goose chase' in *Romeo and Juliet* as a metaphor for hopeless pursuit. Perhaps the phrase is a reflection on Wild Geese, a name given to Irish mercenary soldiers who went to fight in futile European conflicts from the 16th to the 18th centuries. There is still a strong metaphorical connection in the Emerald Isle between migrating grey geese and their worldwide Irish diaspora.

It is a cold October morning at Martin Mere, more than 50 years after my first encounter with the magic of wild geese. The skies are cloudy to the western horizon, and thousands upon thousands of pink-footed geese are coming in at high altitude as if through a cracked layer in the sky from another dimension, from another world – perhaps the alternative universe of Irish Celtic myth. The incoming birds take well over 30 minutes to arrive, descend in wave upon wave, whiffling and honking, tumbling and toppling into fields of weather-worn stubble, their dangerous journey over.

I share this experience with another crusty old birder. We look at each other, speechless. I see him embarrassedly wipe a tear from his right eye, just before I do the same.

On another occasion, well into my senior years, I take a stroll along a rather pleasant footpath near a drainage ditch in Martin Mere. Was this the ditch where I had that close encounter with that splendid barn owl? The memory is strong still, all these years later.

A smart adult male blackbird is frantically busy scattering leaf litter looking for a juicy worm. He interrupts his search when he sees me and gives me the once over, checking I am no threat, before going back to rummage. There's a bench where I can take a rest and watch this fine specimen. We are both conscious of each other: a private stand off between an old human and a beautiful cock blackbird. I am involved in another animal's existence.

The blackbird encounter prompts thoughts of how birds get by in their world. Just how do they interact, how do they see danger, what does it mean to be attentive? Do they indulge in play? What do we mean when we say a bird is conscious? Can a bird be truly conscious?

There are many definitions of consciousness, but there is one among several which works for me, as a naturalist: an ability to see oneself as an individual; to be self-aware.

Behavioural biology has many examples where animals show human-like conscious behaviour. The two groups most often mentioned in this context are cetaceans (whales, dolphins, porpoises) and primates. When we, as humans, look in a mirror we are conscious we are looking at ourselves. Scientists who study animal behaviour have introduced large mirrors to species such as chimpanzees and dolphins and have watched their reactions. We must be careful here how we draw conclusions, as we can't be sure that chimps and dolphins have the same conscious recognition processes that we, *Homo sapiens*, possess; but it's a reasonable assumption, given our brains are so similarly structured and sharing as we do common evolutionary ancestry.

Chimpanzees, when first shown their image in a mirror, take up threatening poses and gestures, as if the image is that of another chimpanzee. After a few days this aggressive behaviour calms down and they start to use the mirror to groom themselves, even pick their teeth and look at parts of their body they had not seen before. Experimenters have marked the faces of chimpanzees with a dot of red dye above one eyebrow and above an ear. When the chimps look in the mirror, using the reflection as a guide, they try to rub out the red dots. This can only mean chimps recognise themselves in the mirror. They are self-aware. This was a breakthrough experiment. There then followed more examples in other species; similarly successful experiments have been conducted with orangutans, gorillas, dolphins and even elephants.

When we see creatures such as dolphins learning to surf, killer whales working as a group to catch their prey, corvids like choughs and ravens clearly playing in family groups, and alpha male ospreys dictating terms over who is to fish first from a lochan, we are seeing examples of self-awareness, a form of consciousness.

The idea that consciousness is not a unique human trait is not new. The evidence for the gradual evolution of the human brain through our ancestral primates is unquestioned. So, it must be argued, consciousness is not necessarily a distinctly human attribute. Thomas Huxley, Darwin's associate, observed:

> The doctrine of continuity is too well established for it to be permissible to me to suppose that any complex natural phenomenon comes into existence suddenly, and without being preceded by simpler modifications; and very strong arguments would be needed to prove that such complex phenomena as those of consciousness, first make their appearance in man.
>
> *Huxley, 1874*

There are two principal ideas as to how consciousness arose in our evolution. It could have appeared suddenly at some point, perhaps when languages first appeared. Alternatively, consciousness was always there, continuous if you will, from the very start in primitive life forms which understood, and were conscious of, their environment.

Constructive and cogent philosophical argument often coalesces around these two opposing views. In the debate around how and when consciousness first emerged, there are those who believe there was a specific point in evolution which triggered consciousness. This group is known as the discontinuity theorists. At a certain point along the evolutionary path, they argue, the consciousness light was switched on. This group finds it difficult, though, to decide at what actual precise point consciousness did come about. Was it the development of language or was it the idea of a theory of mind? Was it the way we learned to manage our environment? The problem with this theory is that it is difficult to identify the precise point in our evolution when indeed the 'lights' of consciousness were actually switched on – but switched on they were, for this view to hold.

Those on the other side of the discussion, continuity theorists, do not of course have this problem. Consciousness is deemed to be part of even the most basic life forms, which innately have a basic awareness of their environment, through to the most complex, self-aware animals we discussed earlier. It is possible that consciousness develops a level of complexity on a gradual sliding scale joining these two extremes on a continuum. Consciousness in this context exists at many levels: it may be very primitive, and language is certainly not a prerequisite. Rather, it is suggested that as life forms evolve and develop, so do their associated conscious experiences. These types of experience are dependent on the life to which they belong, and it is argued that consciousness of a sort was always there, no matter how primitive the experience and the life form. This sort of approach makes sense to me, and has many followers. There is no great 'eureka' moment; consciousness simply evolved as part of the behaviour patterns of evolving biological life forms. When I'm part of nature, waiting patiently for a sanderling to follow the incoming tide or watching a barn owl meticulously and silently quarter a field in search of voles in the evening's fading light, it seems to me a bird's conscious aware-ness meticulously suits its needs.

There is so much evidence that even the most basic life forms are conscious entities. Sentience is another expression of consciousness, and a much-used definition says that sentience is the capacity to feel, perceive or experience subjectively. Eastern philosophy has long maintained that sentience is a metaphysical quality of all living entities. Sentience requires the respect and care of other sentient beings. It is for this reason that Buddhists, for instance, are vegetarian. They have an unquestioning respect for all life forms – yet interestingly, their logic tells them not to have any qualms when eating an animal which has died of natural causes.

Simply grasping the idea of consciousness for all sentient animals has many consequences for so much of our interaction with other animals. What should we eat? Should we become vegetarians? How should we rear livestock? Should we have battery chickens, cattle from industrial production, farmed salmon? If we treat all animals as conscious beings, then our attitudes to nature and our environment are changed fundamentally – and, may I offer, for the better. Nature becomes part of our collective, interrelated biology, and looking after nature becomes the end as well as the means.

At the age of 23 I found myself working for a big chemical company on Teesside. There's a beach in Redcar, where I lived. Folk used to regularly collect lumps of dislodged coal from an open seam on this beach, and it was here I found a guillemot, struggling to survive, his breast feathers covered in thick, black crude oil.

I use the masculine for Guillie. I'm not sure of the bird's gender, but I always thought of the bird as male. Perhaps it was his stubborn nature. I took Guillie home, cleaned and fed him. He was very weak at first and I had to force-feed him the best cod and haddock until he managed to gobble down the pieces himself. I think it took no more than a couple of weeks for him to get his natural oils back up to the level needed to give him back his natural buoyancy. When he was ready to be released, I returned him to the very same beach, with some trepidation. I did not want him to swim back into an oil slick.

I took him to the water's edge and sat him on the tide line. We were completely alone on the beach and the light was fast disappearing. He looked around and swam off a few yards, stopped and swivelled his head and looked back at me for a good minute. To this day, this rational, evidence-driven old bloke still grapples with the idea of Guillie wanting to say thanks when he turned around and looked me in the eye for a good 60 seconds. The scientist in me tells me I am indulging in pure, unadulterated anthropomorphism, but the experience haunts me still. I'm sure he knew. Perhaps Guillie did take conscious time out before heading off into the waves.

15

MIGRATE

Aristotle (384–322 BCE) notes that his local crane populations migrate in winter. Cranes are big birds, easily spotted flying south in large groups: 'vismig' or visual migration, to use current birding jargon. Aristotle also sees, in autumn, swallows feeding on the insect life above ponds before they suddenly disappear. Here one day, gone the next. He knows that other species of small animals, like bats, hibernate, so he attributes the sudden departure to hibernation – presumably, he writes, in holes and cavities, near those ponds where he sees them feeding. It is perhaps surprising to our minds that Aristotle did not extend the known idea of migrating cranes to other birds such as swallows.

Why do birds, and other animals, migrate? The easy answer is 'in search of a reliable meal for themselves and their young'. Locating predictable and plentiful food sources, where predation is not a major problem, is the major determinant for migration.

Just as farmers take their sheep off the mountains in winter and move them to warmer lower pastures with more grass, so some bird species move short distances looking for food as cold winter conditions move in. Hen harriers breed in our upland moorlands – or to be more precise, if left alone by those managing estates for grouse – hen harriers breed *successfully* in our uplands. Come wintertime, these beautiful raptors leave the high ground and move to warmer conditions along our coasts and particularly in our estuaries, like the Dee.

There is a similar vertical migration which occurs in our oceans. Mediterranean fishermen know the catch of species such as anchovies is far better at night. During the Second World War, when submarines were deployed their sonars picked up massive echoes which looked exactly like the ocean floor but at a depth of only 1,500 feet or so. They were shoals of fish. Submarines would even try to hide in these shoals. Biologists have confirmed that these echoes were indeed from marine life (krill, larvae of all sorts, and copepods) which rise to the surface at night and descend again the following morning. The vertical distance travelled by these minute animals in order to get their breakfast is enormous considering their size.

Once daylight arrives, many fish will descend to the lower, darker depths to avoid predation. Of course, food is scarce or non-existent at these depths. Visibility is poor, but predation is less likely. They return to the surface to feed at night.

For this very reason, osprey fish mostly efficiently at dawn, catching their prey shortly before suitable fish return to deeper waters after a night's feeding near the surface. Indeed, ospreys prefer to fish in shallow water, as their prey cannot escape by descending to the depths. Like many birds who depend on fish and other marine life they have also evolved white underparts, which make them less visible to their prey. Think gulls, think terns, think auks, think most species of duck.

Spectacular winter starling murmurations, just before they descend into their favourite reed-bed roosts, are made more dramatic by the massive influx of starlings from our northern continental neighbours whose winters are much harsher than ours. Irruptions of birds like waxwings, bramblings and hawfinches in our gardens, woods and churchyards occur when Scandinavian winters are particularly brutal.

The east coast of England, from Northumberland to Norfolk, provides excellent opportunities to watch this autumn migration. One place attracts birders from all over the north of England: Spurn Point, a narrow spit of dunes and fields which guard the Humber Estuary. In the right conditions, mixed flocks of thrushes and finches will fly in at around 500 feet, and occasionally the odd bird will plummet like a stone to land with a *whoosh!* in a nearby bush.

Goldcrests, our smallest bird, arrive exhausted from their journey over the North Sea, weighing in at around 6 grams – that's the weight of one and half small sugar cubes. It is difficult not to walk on these fine little fellers as they recover by grubbing for food along paths, coppices and green lanes.

Along the same east coast, particularly at the sea cliffs off Bamborough and Filey, colonies of puffins, guillemots and razorbills provide another example of migration. For many years we had no idea where these birds went during winter. It was always assumed they spent their winters out at sea, but where exactly? How far did they travel? If we are going to protect these birds, we need more details of their lifecycles.

Puffins, or to give them their full moniker, Atlantic puffins, breed throughout the North Atlantic. Our islands are at the southern end of their breeding range. They come ashore to breed in April and have gone by July, spending their winter in the seas around the North Atlantic. A window of just four months to raise a single chick or puffling.

A team of naturalists fitted geolocators to the legs of over 50 puffins from our North Sea east coast. These tiny devices weigh only 1.5 grams, less than 0.4 per cent of the puffins' body weight. The results from these gadgets were remarkable. It transpires most of these birds travel far into the North Atlantic, to a sea area equidistant from Iceland and Scotland. However, a small proportion stay locally and use the North Sea as their winter base. This research also shows that their breeding success can be attributed to their choice of wintering grounds: factors such as distance travelled and food availability are key to the bird returning to the breeding colony in good enough condition to successfully raise a single chick.

Guillemots, on the other hand, do not to go to such lengths during winter. Their migrations take them to no more than 300 kilometres offshore, spreading out south and west from their nesting sites.

Many birds migrate much longer distances than simply travelling offshore to the ocean wilderness. Our own patch, along the north Wirral shoreline, offers many examples of wading birds such as dunlin, sanderling, knot and godwits that breed in the Arctic and spend their winters in our milder climate. The same goes for pink-footed geese and whooper swans, which we as young lads found wintering in the dormant Lancashire potato fields at Martin Mere.

Quite how these migratory patterns first evolved is still an unclear area of zoology, but informed conjecture suggests it is likely these migratory practices developed to follow a specific diet. Evolution led to highly developed physiological differences in birds' bills to exploit ecological niches, which meant that species have to move where their preferred food can be found. Evolved bill design, as we read earlier, is a major factor in limiting menu choice. Seasonal changes affect what's on the menu, so birds will slowly extend their range to follow their niche nutrition.

Summer visitors such as hirundines (swallows and martins) and many warblers make the dramatic desert crossing from sub-Saharan Africa in our spring. Once across the Sahara, they take one of two principal routes. Either east through the Bosphorus, or west, across the Strait of Gibraltar and via southern Spain. It has been calculated as many as 400 million birds use the western route where the sea crossing, at its minimum, is just 15 kilometres.

Why do these birds leave the food abundance of Africa's equatorial regions and risk everything to fly across the Sahara? It is thought that if all birds were to stay in the same tropical regions all year round, food would become scarce and breeding would be less successful. As food sources regenerate in the North each spring, millions of birds migrate to those areas to take advantage of this cyclical abundance. As food supplies dwindle by autumn, they return to the tropical regions which have, in the meantime, been replenished. This is a high-risk journey, and many do not make it. Mortality is as high as 40 per cent in several passerine species whose young birds, born in Europe, make the trip across the Sahara for the first time in our autumn.

Some species migrate over quite short distances. A fine example is the robin. The birds we see in winter could well have come over from Scandinavia, and the birds we see in summer might well have come to us from further south. We are unlikely to see the same robin come to our garden feeders throughout the year.

How do birds know their migration routes? Evolution has played its part, as not all birds use the same navigational tools. Some use the sun and stars to find their way to their breeding or wintering grounds, others learn the relevant landmarks taught them by their parents. Studies have shown that a few species clearly use our network of main roads, even using roundabouts. Incredible but true.

If the sky is overcast nocturnal migrants will hold back, indicating that they use a form of celestial navigation. Similarly, the position of the sun will help give birds such as swallows their bearings. But on cloudy days some types of birds can still navigate and fly across the ocean where there are no landmarks. How can they do this?

Scientists have come to believe these seabirds, like shearwaters, monitor the earth's magnetic field using molecules of a mineral called magnetite located in their beaks or possibly their eyes. The iron-containing mineral might well act like a compass. Other scientists think the birds can perceive, or at least register, the earth's magnetic field with their eyes. There is even research in the world of quantum biology which is discovering how the migrating birds use the world of quantum mechanics.[48]

When birds with long migration routes, such as shearwaters, are taken away from their normal environment and introduced to a place which is not part of their known world, they adjust and find their goal. Experiments on Manx shearwaters have shown that they reach their breeding grounds in the Irish Sea even if taken hundreds of miles to places where they never normally travel, such as the eastern Mediterranean. Quite how they do this we do not know. To be able to accomplish this feat they must first determine their new location and then, using whatever navigational tools they have at their disposal, reach their destination.

The *timing* of migration in individual bird species is a different thing altogether. The decision of when to set off on an annual migration can be life-threatening. Get the timing wrong by a few weeks' delay and they will be too late to successfully rear their young before winter sets in; depart too soon and their offspring will be born before the local food

---

48   Jim Al-Khalili and Johnjoe McFadden's book by the title *Life on the Edge: The Coming of Age of Quantum Biology* was published in 2014. Both are professors at the University of Sussex. Jim Al-Khalili is well known for his promotion of science on both Radio 4 and BBC television. He's a leading theoretical physicist, and Johnjoe McFadden is professor of molecular genetics with a particular focus on TB, of all things. This book looks at the new and fascinating world of quantum biology where the weird and wonderful world of quantum mechanics, what happens at the sub-atomic particle level, provides answers to many unanswered questions in biology. One such topic is well covered in the book and this is how birds like the Manx shearwater migrate over vast oceans without landmarks and without the stars to guide them on overcast nights. I guess, like everyone who reads quantum mechanics, you will find it a difficult subject to grasp because it is so counter-intuitive. I for one find that a huge stumbling block, but you must accept the outcomes otherwise it's difficult to make progress

supply is at its optimum. This is especially so for larger birds, like swans or raptors.

In temperate climes there are discernible differences in day length, and this is thought to be a trigger to migrate. But what about birds like the osprey, who winter in tropical zones where the day's length is almost constant during the year? How do they know when it is time to head north? We know from experiments with captive birds such as starlings that there is a distinctive and measurable restlessness at the times when their wild peers would be on migration. They must have an internal clock which we do not yet understand. The example of the osprey is further complicated as they will only migrate north in spring if they have reached sexual maturity, which is after two winters in the tropics.

How do birds prepare for migration? Again, nature has evolved the answers. Before their mammoth journey a migrating bird often doubles its body weight by laying down fat reserves. Biological changes also occur to organs such as liver and kidneys, which reduce in size during migration. We know from ringing records of a stunning example of a sedge warbler, which flew 4,000 kilometres without a stopover. This bird weighed 23 grams when he began the journey and only 9 grams when he arrived.

The distance travelled during migration often equates to extreme weight loss and internal organ changes. The bar tailed godwit, for example, which migrates up to 11,000 kilometres, is up to 55 per cent fat on departure whilst its digestive internal organs reduce by 25 per cent during the trip.[49] The bar-tailed godwits we see in Britain have a comparatively easy journey, setting off from northern Scandinavia and Russia on a course between west and south-west, with only the short North Sea crossing to contend with. (*Photo 34*)

Why do some species of birds migrate and others from the same genus do not? One of the questions we asked as young lads in the Lancashire stubble fields was, on the face of it, simple: Why do whooper swans fly back to Iceland in spring when our own mute swans stay put?

---

49   There are three races in involved. The bar-tailed godwits we see in Britain have a comparatively easy journey, setting off from northern Scandinavia and Russia on a course between west and south-west, with only the short North Sea crossing to contend with. Another race, from eastern Russia, head south to the Yellow Sea off China and then on to Australia, and face much longer sea crossings. The star performers, though, are those who breed in Alaska. These birds spend between five and nine days in continuous flight above the Pacific Ocean, ending up in New Zealand. And then, six months later, all the way back again.

Presumably mute swans have a very similar diet to whoopers, as their digestive biology must be almost identical. Mute swans find the necessary food – so why do whoopers fly back to Iceland to breed? We had no easy answer at the time when I was a young lad, but it appears this has more to do with the Arctic's better breeding conditions. The area around the Arctic Circle has a long day length, giving adult birds more time to feed their chicks. An adult whooper swan weighs a whopping 15 kilograms. That means a lot of feeding, and often there are a couple of cygnets to rear. The Arctic tundra is a big place, so there is less competition for food and there is reduced risk of predation.

Pink-footed geese follow the same migration patterns as whooper swans, and for the same reasons. Ospreys also migrate north from the equatorial food abundance of West African countries such as the Gambia in search of long daylight hours to feed their youngsters. Northern regions are abundant in food in the summer, and those long days are crucial if they are to feed their chicks enough for them to become fully grown adult birds.

Migration is a most complex subject, and there is no one rule for all species. Migratory birds have evolved in the most extraordinary and varied ways, and we are still discovering new aspects to this complex subject. Perhaps we can state that birds simply have instincts to migrate which are totally deterministic. They may well learn from their parents (nurture) but instinct prevails (nature).

I'm walking the coastline from Leasowe to West Kirby. It's a summer's day, and my 65th birthday approaches. The calm sea carries those remembered blue-green hues, turning dark navy and then teal greens as the light changes.

Am I too migrating? Not in space but in time?

There's that old Leasowe lighthouse, now on my left. My right knee is playing up; there's no need to clamber down the embankment. I came here only six months ago. It won't have changed.

What I do recall from my youth are feelings of an intimate sense of place. I'm surrounded by key loci of old. The shoreline, the groynes, the footpaths, the market gardens, the rakes. I could go on.

What is missing is the sunken forest off Meols, now hidden under those shifting sandbanks.

As I am walking alone, slowly, along this shoreline with Liverpool's container port cranes behind me, the hills of North Wales ahead show their soft purples and blues in the humid air. It is good to be here, alone with my thoughts. A few curlews peel off the rocky groyne and fly back to their pasture meadows. An oystercatcher leaves and pipes out his call. A lone cormorant passes out at sea, low over the water, heading for Hoylake.

All is as before. Nature is reassuringly here to be enjoyed. We can record in detail her taxonomy, but she's an elusive mistress in her totality. 'Nature is surely everything?' I ask myself. 'Just accept this world around me. We don't need explanations of this mystery.' An inner peace descends like a soft blanket. This instant. There's a calm stillness out here on the meadow pastures, the carrs of Meols.

As too often happens in such meditative moments, the spell is broken. This time a ringing bicycle bell. I step aside to let the rider through.

16

PROGRESS?

Today Leasowe Shore is part of the North Wirral Country Park. Burton and Parkgate Marshes are now a flourishing RSPB reserve, Loggerheads is another country park, and Hilbre is owned by Wirral Borough Council, which employs a full-time ranger to look after the wildlife. Martin Mere is now a major centre of conservation undertaken by the Wildfowl & Wetlands Trust (WWT). The patches we went to as young lads are thankfully now part of a conservation network administered by various bodies.

The WWT offers a great example of what first-class conservation work can do. It is their goal to save and create valuable wetlands within the United Kingdom, predominantly around our coasts. They also hold dear the philosophy that we as individuals must connect with nature.[50]

It is true that when we find nature we often find ourselves.

Today there are nine reserves in the WWT's portfolio, stretching from Somerset to Washington on Wearside. All are of major international importance for migrating birds coming here for their winter months or using our shores to breed.

The provenance of these reserves goes back to a remarkable guy called Peter Scott. His father, Captain Scott, had led the fatal expedition to the South Pole in 1912. Peter grew up in a wealthy family, and after his time at Cambridge he could indulge his passions. One of them was to explore the

---

50   https://www.wwt.org.uk/

country's wild marshes to admire wintering flocks of wildfowl. Another passion was to paint wildfowl. By 1946 he had opened a reserve on the upper reaches of the River Severn near Slimbridge in Gloucestershire, and called it the Severn Wildfowl Trust. He established the red lists of critically endangered birds, and started implementing conservational programmes to protect birds such as the nene or Hawaiian goose, when only 30 remained in the wild. He soon had the population back to 2,000, and invited BBC TV into his own home for live programmes from Slimbridge. He kick-started the BBC's exemplary take on wildlife with a series called 'Look'. A young David Attenborough featured on his show too – but most of all Peter Scott communicated his conservation message so well with his audience. Ideas on protecting our environment were brought directly into our homes.

Martin Mere was opened in 1975 to protect and conserve the pinkfeet and whooper swans, and by 1999 the WWT had opened another reserve, at Caerlaverock on the Solway Firth, which helps provide long-term protection of the overwintering Svalbard barnacle geese in the firth. The population has now reached 25,000 after dropping to just 300 in 1948; another environment protection success.

When bird conservation is discussed, we think of the Royal Society for the Protection of Birds as the natural centre for all matters concerning bird protection and conservation. It has been an incredible success story. There are over 500,000 paid-up members, and nearly 200 RSPB reserves throughout the UK. For me as a young birder in the 1960s, its then new reserve at Minsmere in Suffolk, took on almost mythical status: if you wanted to see avocets and marsh harriers, you had to go to Minsmere. And now, both species can be seen at many locations around the UK.

The RSPB evolved from the Society for the Protection of Birds (SPB), formed in 1889 by Emily Williamson in Didsbury, Manchester. Its aim was to prevent the slaughter of birds whose feathers were used in the late Victorian period to adorn ladies' hats. At the time the SPB was an all-ladies affair, and it was an instant success with many women, including Queen Victoria. By 1903 it was producing a regular newsletter called 'Bird Notes and News', and by 1904, having received its royal charter, it had become the RSPB, as we know it today.

Its first nature reserve was purchased in Romney Marshes in 1930 (this was sold in 1950) but it opened its flagship reserve at Minsmere in 1947, and many more followed. Along the way it took up the cudgels to fight oil companies over spillages, objected to planning applications if it was seen that breeding bird populations would suffer and began local bird protection initiatives such as the ospreys at Loch Garten and many more.[51]

A third conservation group is the Wildlife Trust. There are 47 distinct Wildlife Trusts, most organised by county, which do their best to protect wildlife in their area. A quick look at their website shows the individual reserves in alphabetical order. Counting all the sites under A tells me there are nationally 73 sites; B has 209. I give up trying to get a national total, but you get the picture. There are lots. They run into the thousands. Most are small plots, just a few acres, but others, like the 500-acre Brownsea Island in Dorset, come in at over 100 acres.

The trust's history goes back to May 1912, when a polymath of a guy, Nathaniel Charles Rothschild (1877–1923) known as Charles, with powerful connections through his banking family, held a meeting with three other like-minded colleagues (Charles Edward Fagan, William Robert Ogilvie-Grant and Francis Robert Henley) to found the Society for the Protection of Nature Reserves (SPNR).

Their plans and ideas looked at the macrocosm in nature and tried to lay out top-down strategies to protect nature. Their overarching desire was to leave nature well alone and let it thrive 'naturally'. So very wise and prescient for the time. Within three years they had drawn up and published 284 suitable sites for this initiative within Britain and Ireland. It is fair to say that this list was the catalyst for the conservation measures brought in by the state after the Second World War, notably the National Parks and Access to the Countryside Act of 1949.

Whilst these four wise men were thinking of national conservation strategies, local wildlife conservation groups were in their early days. The first was in Norfolk in 1926, followed by another in Yorkshire in 1946 and Lincolnshire in 1948. Many more were opened during the 1950s, and the

---

51 *Mrs Pankhurst's Purple Feather: Fashion, Fury and Feminism – Women's Fight for Change.* Tessa Boase's book is a very good read indeed; it covers the beginnings of the RSPB and a protest against the trade in exotic birds to decorate ladies' hats.

SPNR became the umbrella organisation to manage these proliferating local trusts. The Scottish Wildlife Trust was formed in 1964, and Ulster followed in 1978.

There is another conservation organisation which holds more acres than all the rest put together. The National Trust. If one includes the National Trust for Scotland, it is responsible for 815,000 acres of land, farmed by around 2,000 tenants. Contrast that with the RSPB's ownership of 323,000 acres.

The ideas behind establishing the National Trust can be traced back to the introduction of the 1773 Enclosure Act, passed during the reign of George III. This law enabled the enclosure of common land whilst at the same time removing the right of commoners' access, which had been used for many generations. At the time the House of Commons was almost entirely constituted of land-owning MPs, and the House of Lords was entirely made up of landowners. A mighty selfish stitch-up, you might say. By 1845 a total of 6.5 million acres had been appropriated by the country's landowners, including 3 million acres of common and waste lands. The loss of rights to common lands meant real hardship to landless folk.

But then in 1865 an organisation known as the Commons Preservation Society (CPS) was established, with two main aims. Firstly, to promote the idea that green open spaces should be open to the public, and secondly, to address the loss of individuals' rights to common land. It attracted the support of thinkers like John Ruskin and John Stuart Mill, the latter a Liberal MP. There then followed 30 years of legal battles to prevent further enclosures, including Epping Forest. Eventually an organisation with specific responsibilities to manage properties in the public interest, the National Trust, was set up in January 1895 by three influential and far-sighted individuals: Sir Robert Hunter, Octavia Hill and Canon Hardwicke Rawnsley.

However, there is no mention of nature conservation as a remit for the original National Trust. It was there to look after and manage landed estates and their properties whilst providing access to these areas for the general public, for their spiritual well-being. It is an honourable intent, and is very popular today – but quite different from those of the RSPB, WWT and the Wildlife Trusts. Of late it is fair to say National

Trust thinking has broadened to include nature conservation and environmental protection projects, but old habits die hard.[52] Testament to this was the organisation's decision to continue to allow trail hunting (which can so easily kill foxes 'by accident') on its land: *Sunday Telegraph*, 22 October 2017.[53]

It is unthinkable that the RSPB, WWT or Wildlife Trusts would have even contemplated such an idea.

Leaving aside the National Trust's provenance in the shires and its perceived patrician attitudes, the picture I'm trying to put across is that environmental protection and conservation efforts are healthy and active. The RSPB, WWT and Wildlife Trusts have done well to protect unique habitats, and the work must – and will – continue.

Despite a few disasters, we have successfully protected many of UK's important biodiverse sites with a plethora of nature reserves. These sites are testament to the great work of many conservation naturalists, often in difficult circumstances. However, these refuges are oases surrounded by often-sterile farmland, with little chance of providing a long-term model of interconnected wildlife conservation.

We live in a densely populated island where most farms are managed intensively with little or no regard for wildlife. Our nature reserves have become small pockets of biodiversity, isolated from each other by man-made barriers to wildlife: our vast road network, railway lines, towns, cities, rural housing estates, business parks and so on.[54]

Now we can add the devastating insulating effect of our industrialised farming business.

Our efforts in the UK to protect our natural environment have been piecemeal at best and dysfunctional at worst. Unless we tackle, head

---

52 'The National Trust has bought 460 acres (186 hectares) of farmland in the Peak District in a bid to help wildlife. A total of 198 acres (80 hectares) has been purchased at High Fields in Stoney Middleton, alongside another 262 acres (106 hectares) bought at Greensides near Buxton. It is the biggest farmland acquisition by the trust since it bought Trevose Head in Cornwall in 2016. The money came from legacies left by supporters.' BBC News website, 7 July 2018.

53 https://www.pressreader.com/uk/the-sunday-telegraph/20171022/281560881035043

54 Although roads and railways have for many years created barriers, Plantlife, a plant conservation charity based in Salisbury, has recognised that their verges can make wonderful wildlife corridors, and is successfully encouraging local councils to restrict their trimming and slashing: https://plantlife.love-wildflowers.org.uk/roadvergecampaign

on, the economic model used by our farming community, there is little chance for our environment.

Farmers are subsidised by taxpayers to provide low-cost foodstuffs, but our farms, so important in connecting all our nature reserves, are largely sterile, monoculture deserts where few insects and birds prevail. Field systems of single crops are the norm – and, worryingly, farmland accounts for an estimated 43 million acres or roughly three-quarters of all our UK land mass.

We may think of farming land as wild and full of nature, but unfortunately it is simply not the case. There is so much evidence that the intensive practices needed to increase productivity to supply food at globally competitive prices have drastically reduced wildlife populations which once survived and co-existed on farmed land. I can offer many examples in the bird world, but I mention just a few. When I was birding as a lad, corn burnings, yellowhammers, grey partridge, lapwings and skylarks were common. Not any more. Scientific studies suggest that drastic changes in agricultural practices significantly contribute to this situation.

Modern agricultural practices have led to the systematic removal of hedgerows, which has been catastrophic to wildlife. Hedgerows form wildlife corridors joining woodlands, ponds and other wildlife hotspots. Studies show 99,000 miles of hedgerow were removed in the UK between 1950 and 1995. This figure is thought to be one half of all our hedgerows – removed in order to increase field size, so farms could benefit from economies of scale, the more efficient use of larger farm machinery. Such vast open fields did not exist in the UK 50 years ago.

Other changes to agricultural practices which damage our natural environment include winter sowing of wheat and barley,[55] less hay and more silage,[56] and the intensive use of pesticides.

---

55 A total of nine studies from Denmark, Sweden and the UK looked at the effects of sowing crops in spring or autumn on farmland wildlife. Five studies (including one replicated controlled trial, and a review) found that planting crops in spring rather than autumn resulted in higher numbers of farmland birds, weed diversity or weed density, whereas winter wheat and barley led to lower biodiversity.

56 Silage runoff liquor is one of the strongest pollutants that occurs on farms. It's at least 200 times stronger than untreated domestic sewage, so even in very small quantities its effects are devastating. Some farmers are improving their silage storage facilities, often as a result of local pollution alert reports generated by members of the national riverfly monitoring scheme: https://www.riverflies.org.

Of all those practices, the biggest – by far – contributors to our overwhelming loss of biodiversity, a principal culprit, are the massive doses of pesticides we apply on those prairie-like fields where hedgerows have long disappeared. A recent study on insect life is truly alarming. We have lost 75 per cent of our insects in the last 27 years. If you think this is an exaggeration, then think on. When we drive in our cars on fine summer days, we hardly ever see an insect splattered on our windscreen. Twenty years ago, after an evening's drive, a windscreen would be covered, literally, in their mortal remains. A second stark indicator is the fact that whereas until the 1960s flocks of gulls could frequently be seen following the plough in the full expectation of dinner being turned up for them, now very few, if any, bother to do so. The soil is dead.

The evidence for this massive decline is not just anecdotal; it comes from detailed and comprehensive data which has been collected from many sources, including some nature reserves in north-west Europe, which have recorded the destruction of 75 per cent of their insect populations since 1990. Clearly, the loss of insect life cannot be down to the reserves and has to be attributed to the practices of the farms that surround them.

There is no reason to suggest that the UK's farming practices or our management of nature reserves are any different from those of our neighbours. What is worrying is the huge impact this loss of insect numbers will have, as they make up two-thirds of all life on Earth. If we lose enough insects all the ecosystems will collapse.

It's not as if we even need massive doses of pesticides. Many studies show that these chemicals, costly as they are, do not deliver profit-per-hectare in the long run; but the power of the 'big pharma' lobby is huge.[57] Many, but thankfully not all, farmers tend to become addicted to the use of pesticides, and feel they cannot run the risk of not using whatever is promoted as the latest 'discovery'. It is hardly fair to highlight one chemical company, as they are all equally culpable, but Monsanto produced many chemicals which have since been banned, including: DDT, cancer-causing polychlorinated biphenyls (PCBs), and Agent Orange, used in Vietnam

---

57 Bayer bought Monsanto for $66 million in 2018. It will be retaining its product brands but retiring the Monsanto name. It's so tarnished. Even more power to the Bayer lobby. Subsequent commentary suggests this was one of the worst buy-outs in the world of big pharma.

as a defoliant. The message, however, applies to the lot of them, including Bayer, Dow and Dupont.

The next time you see these claims, made by big pharma and their sophist friends in public relations, think again.[58]

The common claim is that we cannot live without pesticides as, without them, we could not feed the growing population of the Earth. When we hear that claim it is often to defend modern agriculture as we know it; we tend to think of the vast prairie wheat fields of the richer developed nations which provides our 'daily bread'. But when you look at the total picture of our planet, most of the world's food production comes from small farmers who cannot afford pesticides.

Another claim is that pesticides are not so dangerous. There is so much evidence coming to light which disproves this claim. It does take time however for such evidence to come to light. Organophosphates, DDT and atrazine all had claims to be safe when they were first sold and marketed. They are now banned. Glyphosate, the active ingredient in Roundup, has been classified as a probable carcinogen by the International Agency for Research on Cancer. But it can still be bought at your local garden centre.

As individuals we rely on our government to protect us from such harmful chemicals. If that is the case then why do big pharma spend so much on lobbying to get governments around the world to see it their way.

The protection of our environment at the micro level, at the level of the local nature reserve, has no defence whatever against massive agricultural pesticide spraying – or, indeed, against our global climate crisis.

Modern, intensively farmed Britain has turned great swathes of what was once mixed farming of hedged open countryside into sterile, single-crop manufacture. Whether it's the swaying wheat fields of Cambridgeshire, the strangely noiseless conifer plantations of the Forestry Commission, the acres of farmed daffodils in Fenland or the massive fields of yellow rape for its seed, the situation is grim indeed. What has happened to our insect population is an ecological catastrophe.

---

58   For more information, look up EcoWatch, a community of experts publishing quality science-based content on environmental issues and causes, and solutions for a healthier life and a healthier planet: https://www.ecowatch.com/

Intensive farming is leaving all our nature reserves as increasingly isolated pockets of reducing biodiversity suffering from the effects of the agribusinesses' use of pesticides. Open, mixed, organic farms should be the connecting network joining all our nature reserves, providing corridors where insects thrive.

Mark Cocker in his excellent book, *Our Place*,[59] tells the tale of Raveningham Hall's 5,500-acre estate in Norfolk where an integrated approach to farming and protecting nature's needs has worked so well. The 3,500-acre Knepp Estate in West Sussex is another example of a successful rewilding programme where farming is organic and profitable and where wildlife has made a great comeback. In just over a decade, Knepp has also seen astonishing results in biodiversity. It is now a breeding hotspot for purple emperor butterflies, turtle doves and 2 per cent of the UK's population of nightingales.

At the global level much work has been done by Unesco to identify and manage key biodiversity areas around the globe. We can see many success stories such as the minimising of ecotourism at the important Galapagos Islands so as not to disturb this important centre of biodiversity. However, progress overall is poor, and there are far too many examples where human activities still decimate wildlife.

Let's pause for a second and look at just one tragic example.

Through deforestation to plant palm oil as a biomass fuel source we are wreaking havoc in the Borneo forests, decimating orangutans by restricting their breeding range. A paper written in 2018 and presented in the journal Current Biology, states the world lost nearly 150,000 orangutans from the island of Borneo in the past 16 years due to habitat loss and killing, and is on track to lose another 45,000 by 2050.

How do we work out these figures? Between 1999 and 2015 scientists observed 36,555 orangutan nests across Borneo, an island shared between the nation states of Indonesia, Malaysia and Brunei. During this period of 16 years, researchers reported a steep decline in the number of nests they encountered over a given distance: the encounter rate more than halved, from 22.5 nests per kilometre (36 per mile) to 10.1 nests per kilometre.

---

59 *Our Place: Can We Save Britain's Wildlife Before It's Too Late?* by Mark Cocker. A more thoroughly researched, cogent and well written piece on the threats to our wildlife will be difficult to find. It is a must read for anyone who cares about protecting our environment.

That decline, they calculate, represents an estimated population loss of 148,500 individual Bornean orang-utans. Unfortunately, this is just one of many horror stories of global deforestation activities.

This is one example of the carnage that is happening now – but there are success stories, like Knapp Farm, which warrant a justified, if cautious, optimism. We can reverse the trend. The model used at Knapp has worked successfully at the nature reserve at Oostvaardersplassen in the Netherlands. If we are to reverse the wanton destruction of wild habitats, we need to celebrate and publicise each little victory.[60]

Another recent victory was the banning of neonicotinoid insecticides. When these petrochemicals are ingested by bees, the globe's great pollinators, the decline in bee populations is much faster than would otherwise have been the case. An example: bee species feeding on oilseed rape, which is covered by the insecticide neonicotinoid, are three times more likely to be decreasing in numbers. The insecticide 'causes losses of bee biodiversity' in the future, the study from the NERC Centre for Ecology and Hydrology says. The EU banned them in open fields, effective from end 2018.

But sadly it did not quite work that way. An analysis conducted by *Modern Farmer i*n March 2021 found that 205 'emergency derogations' have been granted across member states for the four banned neonicotinoids since 2016.[61]

In 2020 the UK Government passed into legislation a bill which outlines how the European Union's Common Agricultural Policy will be replaced with a new Environmental Land Management scheme. It states that farmers and landowners in England will no longer be paid based on the amount of land they own and will instead be rewarded for improvements made which deliver on restoring natural environments,

---

60   There's an independent publication dedicated to doing just that, in relation to not just wildlife but many more forms of counterbalance to the pessimistic offerings of the mainstream media: *Positive News*, https://www.positive.news/.

61   This is because EU regulation on pesticides has built-in wriggle room. Article 53 of the regulation gives EU member states the right to grant what is called an emergency derogation. This lets member states temporarily authorize banned products for a period of up to 120 days if "such a measure appears necessary because of a danger which cannot be contained by any other reasonable means."

For some, Article 53 provides essential flexibility when faced with difficult weather conditions and pest outbreaks. For others, it is simply a legal loophole used to keep outlawed chemicals in European fields.

achieving more sustainable farming methods consistent with zero carbon emissions by 2050. Farmers will now be rewarded for the recovery of large-scale landscape and ecosystems. The Sustainable Farming Incentive scheme will pay farmers to manage their land in an environmentally sustainable way.

It has been dubbed 'public money for public good'. This is a radical overhaul of the way we dish out subsidies to farmers, and to be welcomed. However, as in all these schemes the devil, as they say is, or will be, in the detail. At the time of writing, it is proposed that 5,000 farmers will be involved in a three-year trial of the scheme, starting late in 2021 – and getting the detail right is going to be crucial. For instance, we do not want to see any wiggle room for those farmers or landowners who want the subsidy but are not prepared to improve their patch for the public good. We don't want a repeat of the multiple flouting of the neonicotinoids bans.

To be positive, this scheme could help the farming community wean its way off its massive and costly dependence on big pharma's insecticides and pesticides. We do know nature has remarkable powers of recovery. Our islands are littered with many examples. Remember the little pub in Brynamman, at the beginning of this book, with its shrub-infested old veranda and the fire-damaged derelict building next door, now a host to sycamore saplings, wrens and house sparrows and all sorts of invertebrate life.

If we give nature a helping hand, she will not let us down. It can be done.

17

SOUL VESSELS

It's July 2018. On a rainy Monday in North Uist in the beautiful Outer Hebrides, after severe storms have battered the island on the previous Saturday night, I wander through several art exhibitions in Taigh Chearsabhagh,[62] an arts centre in Lochmaddy.

One display in particular catches my eye. I stand there, transfixed by an array of carefully laid out, gently coloured ceramic rowing boats of varying sizes, mostly 15 centimetres or thereabouts, all in the same simple, symmetrical, stretched bowl-like shape. There's a hint of the traditional Viking design but no raised prows or afterdeck, no holes for oars, no single mast. I walk around the exhibit looking at these boats from all directions and in all lights. The ceramic in part is translucent, ghostly. Soft colour washes of greys and browns swirl and merge like ink droplets diffusing in cloudy water. There is immense joy at simply looking but this is not enough, I want to touch them but dare not. I want to hold and cradle them like a newborn and stroke them with deep affection brought on by a clean, uncluttered sense of humility. Here is a wonderful piece of art which talks to me directly.

---

62 From the exhibition's brochure: 'Taigh Chearsabhagh was built in 1741 by Neil MacLean (a merchant) … as a traveller's inn. It was one of the first businesses in North Uist to have a slate roof. In 1802 a post office was established in Lochmaddy and is believed to have been in Taigh Chearsabhagh – we still have a post office here today. Sometime after 1900 the building became a house and then later a workshop for the North Uist Estate, and in 1993 it took on new life as the Museum and Arts Centre.'

I'm drawn to reading the ceramicist's own words, but I try to delay. I don't want to know her intent just yet. I say 'her' out of deference to the undoubted, beautiful, soft femininity of the work. That's not to say I should apply gender stereotyping so blatantly. These ceramic model boats carry so many metaphors in my mind as I stand almost dumbstruck by their ability to communicate with me on so many levels: sailors' collective responsibilities; nature's soft but often brutal caress; the philosophy of beauty in symmetry; the old four elements of earth, air, fire and water; mathematical curves and conic sections.

The display is entitled 'Soul Vessels', and the artist is a local lady by the name of Kirsty O'Connor. These are her words:

> Soul Vessels is inspired by the beautiful wooden boats built by five generations of the Stewart family on Grimsay [an island off North Uist]. It also relates to the mythical significance, in many cultures including the Celtic, of the boat as a carrier of the souls of the dead. It commemorates personal losses, as well as honouring souls lost at sea in their search for a new home, linking the current migration crisis with people having had to leave these shores in the past.

The sign at the art exhibition says 'Please do not touch', but that is exactly what I want to do. Whenever a sign says 'Do not' there's always that urge to disobey: I might be missing out.

For the next six months I pined for one of those ceramic boats – it was almost as if our tactile union had not been consummated – and eventually I bought one as a Christmas present to myself. The boat now sits on my desk and I stroke it often.

What is it about this ceramic boat that hits the nerve? I tried to write down at the time these unconscious feelings. I knew I was missing something special, something which perhaps lay deep in my subconscious.

It was the task of writing this final chapter which helped me finally understand the real allure of the ceramic boat on my desk.

In the early sixties there are just a few bird observatories, always referred to as 'obs', dotted around the country, run by professional wardens. Places for volunteers to watch and record bird migration, with the added spice of spotting a rarity under the supervision of a professional warden. 'Obs' are located on important migration routes around our coast. Bardsey Island is the closest to me, off the Llyn Peninsula in North Wales.

Up until the 1970s Bardsey Island was part of the Newborough Estate. The estate had managed the island for over 200 years and had built the six small farm holdings on the island in the 1800s. In 1973, to pay off Lord Newborough's death duties, the island was sold to the then Hon. Michael Pearson.[63] When it was again put up for sale, in 1976, the members of the Bardsey Bird Observatory along with various local residents set up the Bardsey Island Trust and bought it in 1977 after an appeal supported by the Church of Wales and many Welsh academics and public figures.

In the trust's own words:

> The trust is financed through membership subscriptions, grants and donations, and is dedicated to protecting the wildlife, buildings and archaeological sites of the island; promoting its artistic and cultural life; and encouraging people to visit as a place of natural beauty and pilgrimage.

One or two older Hilbre birders came back from their Bardsey trip with stories of a great birding holiday, the odd 'mega' rare bird and the ringing and recording work of the obs. We – Mac, Roy and I – are hooked. Enquiries are made and plans drawn up to take a trip to Bardsey Island in August. We are going to be staying and working at a bird observatory on a remote island.

We are told to be on the beach at Aberdaron at 11 a.m. on the agreed Saturday morning in August when the local Bardsey farmer, Wil Evans, will arrive to collect us. We are to bring our own provisions for breakfasts and lunches. Obs will provide the evening meal. We three excited youngsters make our way to Pwllheli by Crosville bus from Birkenhead. Another bus gets us to Aberdaron. It is dry. We camp close to the beach, by the side of the small, busy stream.

The sky is pitch black; the new moon offers little. The lights in the nearby village are soon gone. A long way from home. Mac and Roy are

---

63   He was to become 4th Viscount Cowdray in 1995.

16, an anniversary still to come for me, a week away. We settle down for the night to the sound of nearby crashing waves and the lone squeal of an oystercatcher.

Dawn comes too quickly into our thin tents. We have been sleeping in our day clothes in warm sleeping bags. Hungry, we boil, brew and fry. The beach is empty apart from an early dog-walker, reeling gulls and the odd scavenging carrion crow. Repeating waves slowly break, tumble, bubble and decline. The tide is flowing. We wait. It is mid-morning, and the light is good. We had been told by letter to stay on the beach, and if at all concerned to go to the local pub where there might be a message.

Right on time, around the headland an open boat appears, 20 feet long and 6 feet wide, with a man steering an outboard. An oversize rowing boat with a motor. This must be Mr Evans, who farms on the island. The prow thrusts through the low swell and his near-empty boat sits high in the water. We then see another identical boat just behind the first. It is being towed by a length of rope equal to the length of the boat itself.

The boats turn towards the beach and ride the surf until the first eventually beaches. The second is then hauled onto the beach, bow first. These boats normally carry the islanders' supplies and their sheep and cattle to market. Today their coastal trade is three young birdwatchers carrying their hopes and dreams across a couple of miles of ocean to an island they have never seen.

'Morning boys. Ready for the off, are we? You'll have to hang on as I need to collect some supplies from the local shop. Just stay here and look after these two boats.'

It is a calm scene in the bay. After a short time he returns with several bags of shopping and slings them into his boat.

'Now then, you lads, get in this second boat with all your gear. We need as much weight as possible in this boat.'

We climb into the beached boat with our packed rucksacks and our supplies, bought from the same local grocer earlier in the morning. Mr Evans gives us a long oar each. 'Don't worry. It's only if we get close to any rocks, then you can push yourselves off,' he says, smiling.

The beach is empty. No-one to witness our departure. The dog walker has gone. We sit gamely on the cross-thwarts which straddle the vessel. A quick glance to Mac and Roy. We all look at each other and stay silent, trying not to show any fear. Then we are off, dragged by the line wrapped around the prow of our craft. A closer inspection shows the tell-tale holes for rowlocks on the gunwales, testament to the boat's rowing days. I can't swim and there are no life jackets. There is no idle banter.

The sea water here, where the peaty waters from the mountain stream enter the bay, is dark and brackish. As we move into deeper water the colour changes to a mottled green as full salinity returns.

Around the headland we hit the open, deep, blue-green, shining sea. Now, in the heavy swell, the motorised lead boat slows to crest a wave and the towrope slackens. Once the boat has crowned the wave, it picks up speed, sliding effortlessly down the slope, and the rope tightens hard again, pulling our boat violently through the same wave. We lose our balance, and spray is everywhere. This is more than unsettling. It's frightening. After several repeats of this buffeting, we get the hang of it. Look only at the rope and ready ourselves for when it goes taut; learn to anticipate the sudden jerk as we ride through the crest.

Slowly we get time to look around. We see Bardsey for the first time in the distance, 2 miles away to the west. The loaf-shaped, dark mass of the 'mountain'; at 550 feet it's the highest part of the island. There's not much said as we stare at the island looking for more detail, yet keeping an eye on the rope. We know from our Ordnance Survey map that this eastern face is steep.

Strands of floating kelp dot the surface. Churning upwells of changing colours from deep below surround our boat. The sea roils beneath as the two open boats slowly track a course respecting the run of the tide, skirting the bigger eddies and avoiding a large rock in the middle of Bardsey Sound. The sea everywhere is alive. Our boats ride the swells and surges. Mr Evans constantly adjusts the tiller of his outboard to keep to his intended course. It's taken a good half-hour to get here, but eventually we reach calmer waters in the lee of the steep slopes of Bardsey's east coast. We are close to the rocks, where the currents are not so vicious. We gingerly stand up, picking up our oars, ready. Farmer Evans looks back at us and gives us a broad grin, which hints we will be fine now.

We follow the coast, a series of sea-washed vertical slabs with narrow ledges and dark crevices. We track slowly along this eastern edge, not too close to the rocks, where guillemots, razorbills and a lone puffin stare at us from their ledges and outcrops. So different. A fulmar passes overhead, silhouetted against the dark cliffs with stiff wings stretched out to collect every ounce of updraft. (*Photo 35*) Adult kittiwakes ride the same updrafts in their whites and soft greys, wing feathers fingering invisible air currents. A peregrine looks down from her rocky lookout, her vertical pantry to survey.

Steep slopes give way to small grassy plateaux where sheep re-tread narrow paths. Our boats carefully skirt a promontory, Pen Cristin, and for the first time we see the island spread out in front of us. The mountain hides a fertile area of fields bordered by dry stone walls, stretching half a mile or so to the island's west coast and a mile or so to the north. A string of several, low, willowy copses follow a watercourse through these fields, the withies.

Where we are landing is a narrow isthmus. The working red and white-striped lighthouse and its two cottages dominate the south of the island, to our left. Farmer Evans reduces speed and manoeuvres our two boats into a narrow inlet, where we beach. The waiting warden and a few helpers unload our belongings.

'Welcome to Bardsey,' says the warden. 'It's supposedly the home of 10,000 Christian souls. Bardsey is old Norse for "isle of the bard".'

Our gear –three, now damp, canvas rucksacks and three damp and not-so-rigid large cardboard boxes of provisions – is loaded onto a trailer and then hauled by tractor on the island's only vehicular track to the obs. Cristin, the lodge, sits tight against the mountain and looks west across the walled fields and withies. It was a school, last used in 1953, but it's our home now until the end of our holidays, providing we get off the island on schedule. Storms often brew up unexpectedly, delaying departure.

Like all buildings on Bardsey, Cristin is a thick-walled, solid stone structure, with paved slab floors and a slate roof. Our warden gives us a brief tour, shows us where we are to keep our own food supplies – a cold slab in a pantry – and explains our duties. We three share an upstairs room, where we each have a bed and a chamber pot. We have our own sleeping bags but the obs provides blankets and pillows. The single toilet is of the soil variety, privy-style, outside. We are told that after using it we should drop in a handful of sawdust from the mound to cover our traces. The toilet is slopped out daily into a waiting cesspit. Electricity is provided by a diesel generator which is switched off in the evening when everyone retires, around nine. We all have our own torches. We are to make our own breakfast and lunch, but the evening meal is provided, and we share a roster of chores given to us by the warden. Thankfully, none of our chores includes the slopping out.

The Bardsey Bird and Field Observatory has a scientific remit to study and record not just birds but all wildlife and botany on the island. Roy is chuffed. If any one of us is the true naturalist, it is Roy. He began as a young botanist with a keen interest in pond life. His first love has not deserted him. He wants to study zoology one day.

The island is divided into sectors and it's the intention to count and record all birds and animals seen in these sectors every day. We lads, as volunteers, support this activity, but first the warden must check our abilities to identify bird species. He asks a few basic questions to test our skills. I fail miserably on one question of gull identification, but he seems okay with my other answers. He looks at me with a wry smile as if to say 'Well, he's made the effort to get here.'

We have the first afternoon to ourselves and decide to climb the mountain to get a better idea of the island's geography. The mountain is directly behind Cristin. It's a balmy day with a light southerly breeze. A skylark trills its ascent into a pale blue sky as a group of noisy black choughs tumble and frolic above soft, closely grazed grasses and patches of deep fern.

Reaching the summit, we sit and look around. Below us are the steep cliffs we followed in our boats. Roy reminds us these cliffs are off limits – but Mac, as ever, sees them as a challenge. As we look north from our vantage point, the cliffs of the Llyn Peninsula stand erect and remote. Bardsey Sound, which we have just crossed, carries strong tidal currents causing the blue slate-green water to froth and swirl, even on this calm day. The island seems to be adrift in the ocean; we have crossed a significant marine margin. A peaceful windy periphery where visual and oral senses are calmed.

There are no vessels to be seen, and Aberdaron is hidden behind the headland. Over the westward horizon is Ireland, and to the south Cardigan Bay, which reaches all the way down to St Davids. Even here, on this grassy summit, bees are out collecting, butterflies meander in the sunlight, a few beetles wander unconcerned and a stream of red-faced swallows head south.

We are getting accustomed to remote places, but this is different. Few words are spoken. We sit there with our thoughts.

Mac breaks the silence. 'This is for me.' He's not one to boast; he says it in his casual, matter-of-fact way.

'Look out there.' Roy points to a single-masted yacht in the distance, cleaving its way down the channel. 'To be free like that, chasing the wind.'[64]

We sit for a good 20 minutes and decide to move back down to Cristin. I tell my mates I'll follow shortly, and I sit for a while longer on the short grass and look out north.

Isolated once again; those days in the hospital come back to me. The daydream continues. I'm soon talking to Ma, telling her of the journey here, the frightening boat trip across and the climb up the mountain, telling her not to worry, telling her I'll come back safe and well. She promises to visit 'Just like I did when you were in hospital.'

Dawn arrives early, even in August. There is every chance the previous night has brought in new birds. The wind has shifted to a north-easterly, and we understand from the warden that this change often heralds a fall of nocturnal migrants. Mugs of tea brew in the small kitchen and we try our best to be inconspicuous whilst the warden and his team prepare for their daily census.

This morning we are off to the lighthouse for a quick scan of what new birds there might be. It'll be a good hour from Cristin if we include the halts to check every bird. The lane south is high-sided in places. A meadow pipit needs a quick check. Perched on a post with a beak full of insects. A second brood? A stonechat posts sentinel on a gate. A parcel of linnets settle near the track ahead and feed off mature grass seed-heads. A few descend to the puddles on the lane until disturbed by a sleek male sparrowhawk skimming over a stone wall. The hawk also puts up a tinkling flock of goldfinches. (*Photos 36 and 37*)

---

64   Roy followed his dream. In his mid-twenties he single-handedly built a concrete (ferro/cement is the technical term) yacht from scratch in a farmer's yard in Meols. At the age of 27 he sailed off to the West Indies, and as I write these words he is now well on his way to completing his fourth circumnavigation of our globe. He has lived on that boat ever since. Like the top sailor and naturalist that he is, he has chronicled his story: *Around & Around & Around* by Roy Starkey, Paragon 2015. A fine read.

As we approach the narrows the lane's high walls are gone. Our track crosses an open field. On our left is the place where we landed yesterday. The boats have been hauled up on dry land near an old boathouse, and around them sprawls the clutter of fishing paraphernalia. Old ropes, faded pink buoys, stacked lobster pots and pale blue nylon nets lie on the soft turf. An old tractor stands ready for work, but its rusty appearance suggests that might be a struggle.

In the nearby harbour, Henllewyn, grey seals look at us inquisitively. It's low tide and we search kelp-covered rocks for bird life. A curlew looks intent, prodding for breakfast, whilst a much smaller turnstone busies itself in fresh pools. The wind is still blowing gently but it has turned more northerly and carries a slightly colder edge. I recall Mr Evans' remark, 'an easterly wind blows by the hour, but a northerly lasts all day'.

To the right, another bay, Solfach, but this one has a line of rotting kelp drawn out along an almost white sandy beach. Groups of rock pipits crawl amongst the tangled drifts, a few sanderlings patter through rotting detritus. Two mallard drakes take their time to dabble in the shallow water at the tide's edge.

Our target this morning is the lighthouse. After a 15-minute walk along the track we get to the gate in a wall which leads into a large, grassed enclosure surrounding the lighthouse. As we approach we notice the lighthouse is not round but square. Red and white horizontal stripes adorn this 100-foot tower. Propped up against a stone wall are a couple of bikes belonging to the two resident keepers. Their whitewashed cottages are neat and trim. The walled enclosures also have carefully laid-out beds of late summer vegetables. It's a picture postcard scene, framed by an olive-green ocean and cloudless blue sky.

We have been told to respect the privacy of the keeper's cottages, so we look over the walls for any stragglers which have been attracted to the island by the all-night vigil of the powerful searchlight, which can be seen from 25 miles. We look carefully for signs of birdlife. It's quiet, apart from a yellow wagtail on the far side of the enclosure. A beautiful little bird almost head to foot in a shade of buttercup yellow, with a rushing, stop-start gait. It halts for a couple of seconds and strikes a charming pose before catching an insect.

We sit and watch this little piece of sunshine brighten our morning. It's a simple little yellow bird, but why do we find it so beautiful? The colours give it a head start but it's delicate, it's fragile. And then comes the wonder. This little bird will soon migrate thousands of miles to sub-Saharan Africa. There is awe in this feat of endurance, made more sensational by the bird's elegant beauty.

Searching the rest of the gardens we find a couple of willow warblers darting and feeding in low shrubbery. Migrants who made landfall in the night are busy feasting on small insects, building up fat reserves for a few days before they too take off again on their huge migration to sub-Saharan Africa. They are light, ephemeral birds; how on earth do they make the trip?

Our morning is going well. It's just another 15-minute walk to the southern tip of the island, over uneven terrain of tussocks and hidden hollows. A northern wheatear stands proud as it surveys the world. Memories of Hilbre. Creams, whites and blacks, the size of a large robin. These birds are one of the first to arrive in spring and one of the first to leave in autumn. High on Bardsey's mountain northern wheatears breed successfully, but the breeding season is ending so this one looks to be another migrant. It too will soon head off to Africa.

We find a sheltered spot at the island's southern tip, in the lee of the northerly, and scour the dark emerald seascape for passing birds. Visibility is good in the cooler air stream. Hints of glistening lime greens amongst the waves break through white foamy crests. In the troughs, colours revert to deep blues and hints of lilac. A few magnificent gannets head south, forming a line follow-my-leader style, one minute skimming the surface with their wing tips, almost tracing an outline in the heaving swell, the next riding the uplift 20 feet above the surface. We meet one of the assistant wardens, and he explains that these birds will almost certainly be breeding adults from Skokholm, an island off the Pembrokeshire coast in south Wales. They form fishing groups, travelling long distances from their nests to collect food. They ride the ocean's updrafts with hardly a flap of their long, stiff wings. Smaller birds with whirring wings dart low over the waves; guillemots too need to cover long distances to feed before returning to their cliff-face ledge to feed a single chick. By August most chicks have fledged and left.

After an hour's sea watching it's time to walk back following the rugged coastline before meeting the path again at the narrows, which then takes us back to Cristin for a spot of late lunch.

Although youngsters and novices, we are part of a bigger team on Bardsey collecting all this data, a peek into an adult world of birding. The warden and his assistants live on the island from March until November. They get paid to do this. It is their choice. A hobby becomes work.

The early morning light is still soft when we sit down at the narrows to watch, from the precarious privacy of overhanging soft turf, a small mixed wader flock of sanderling, dunlin and turnstones, and a single ringed plover. The flock is 20 feet away, spread out over the small bay of Solfach. A few birds scrape the tidal wrack, others prod the wet sand. One or two preen, but there's a purposeful busyness about the group – petite, clockwork characters in an unfolding drama. We watch carefully, looking for anything unusual in their plumage or behaviour. A tight squadron of half a dozen rock pipits join the group and go straight for the rotting kelp and wrack. These birds blend naturally into the greys, greens and browns of the smelly, tide-washed heap. Four chattering choughs appear from the east and start to dig their own scrapes in the adjacent soft strand, looking for sand flies. Their name was originally onomatopoeic; in old English the letters in 'chough' say 'chiow', exactly their call. One of the four birds has removed so much sand with its red curved beak and red legs that the hollow is deep enough to conceal the bird.

Mallards continue to feed in the low tide's edge, and a cormorant with outstretched wings poses on a nearby rock. I'm with the warden, and he tells me a cormorant's feather structure has evolved for sleek and mobile underwater movement.

'They're expert fishers,' he says, 'but the downside is that their feathers have little bulk and so are less able to repel water. As a result, their feathers absorb more water than those of other diving birds. The evolutionary cost of such underwater skills is the time that's required for them to preen their wing feathers with their body oils and hang them out to dry like washing on a line.'

An alarm call from a turnstone makes the beach group agitated, but after a while they resume foraging. Roy looks up and sees what he thinks is a high-flying peregrine. We train our binoculars, and sure enough it's up there in the high sky, making arc patterns as it climbs. Although we can't be sure, we think it's a tiercel, going by its slim shape and size. He stalls into the wind, hangs firm and looks down with the keenest of eyesight. He glides effortlessly in strong winds, describes tight arcs in a pale blue sky. He rises again high to a dot and then maintains altitude as he moves slowly over towards the waders in the narrows. They can't see him yet. All is calm and peaceful on the beach – and then he stoops. He goes for a straggler, the last of the flock to rise in fright. The dallier is a lone turnstone, and the tiercel – it *is* a male – takes the bird on his first attack and carries off his prey back to the mountain.

We witness nature's economy of death; swift, brutal, necessary. Even though he is the apex bird predator on Bardsey, he is not profligate. Nature has this under control. He has a body weight range of between 300 and 1,000 grammes. Less than 300 grammes and the exertion of hunting will be too much for his frail body; in order to hunt he needs body fat as an energy reserve. But he only takes enough food to maintain body weight: any weight over 1,000 grammes and he loses the agility to hunt successfully. Falconers know this when they train their birds; if they are above a critical body weight they will not come to the lure.

After an evening meal and roll call at Cristin, we wrap up and set off again in the darkening gloom under the guidance of the warden. We are off to the lighthouse again. The sky is overcast and there's every likelihood migrating birds will make for the rotating beam, having lost their ability to navigate by the stars. Handheld torches illuminate our way down the lane, across the narrows and up the path to the lighthouse. As we get close, we see small birds dazzled by the light, many of them hitting the glass lantern and falling stunned to the ground. Dazed small birds are carefully collected from neat gravel paths and grass verges and put into small cloth sacks. The opening to the pouch is drawn tight and the bagged birds are taken back to the obs to be ringed later. Others unseen are high overhead, calling as they travel south.

'Did you hear a little ringed plover?' says the warden.

I'm impressed. There's a heavy nocturnal migration under way, right now, and if it wasn't for the lighthouse we would be none the wiser.

It's getting late, well past midnight. Our warden suggests we try our luck in spotting one of Bardsey's ornithological splendours.

'Go up to Nant, along the track, past Christin, past Carreg Bach, past the cross. Behind the plantation is best. There'll be a few stragglers who are still feeding their chicks. There is no moonlight, so it's ideal.'

The island is home to a breeding colony of around 40,000 Manx shearwaters, one of the largest island colonies dotted around this stretch of the north-west Atlantic Ocean. Shearwaters forage out in the oceans during the day but come back at night to feed their one chick in an underground burrow. We hear their muffled squeaks and weird, wailing calls in the dark. Occasionally we glimpse a pale shape skim by over our heads. We wait with a torch. Greater black-backed gulls and great skuas must also feed their chicks, and will, given the chance, predate shearwaters when they are at their most vulnerable – on land. Darkness provides shearwaters and petrels with cover.

The wait is short. A manxie lands in front of us, 6 yards along the path; it's more of a crash than a deft landing. The bird's anatomy is made for skimming the oceans for months on end, not for a night's brief walk in a dark lane. Its body is 8 inches long from beak to tail. Its legs are positioned underneath a very short tail, making walking a vulnerable, clumsy, rolling shuffle. Within seconds it finds its nest, in this case a burrow underneath one of the large boulders which make up a wall. How on earth does it find its burrow in the pitch-black night?

As with many ocean-going birds, its upperparts are dark brown and underparts are white. When viewed from above their dark plumage merges into the ocean's dark green to provide camouflage from predation. Their white undersides similarly assist when the bird becomes a diving predator for the likes of cephalopods (squid and cuttlefish), crustacea (shrimp, crabs etc) and small fish.

We sit huddled together and wait for more action. It's not long before a whoosh of air is followed by a thud to our left. A torch illuminates a shearwater as it shambles through the coarse grass hillocks to its nest, disappearing into a rabbit-size burrow. Unsurprisingly, shearwaters are found only on islands free of rats and foxes.

The busy world of nature in the dead of night. Sights and sounds we had only dreamed of. Excitedly we return to Cristin, past the old Celtic cross at Nant, near the ruins of the monastery, along the lane and past Carreg Bach, the old farm workers' cottage on the left. The wind rustles a few bushes and shearwater cries are now distant. It's gone 3 o'clock when we make Cristin. A weary climb of those narrow stairs from the kitchen to our room of three beds. No one speaks. Sleep is instant.

A late breakfast the following morning. The warden is alone, sipping his tea. He has already been out on his first census.

'Hi, lads, I have a few minutes spare,' he says. 'How did you get on last night when you went up to Nant? Did you spot any manxies?'

Mac replies, 'Brilliant! We saw five – but it was late, around 2.30, when they came in.'

'Well done. We're very proud of our colony here. Make yourselves a cup of tea, and if you want I can tell you a lot more of these magnificent wanderers.'

Roy makes three mugs and we put them down on the pale green cloth covering the communal kitchen table.

'We think these birds spend the winter down in the South Atlantic, but we're not sure. We have a few ringing records, but we need more information, which is coming in slowly. They also breed on Skomer, a bigger colony than Bardsey's. They arrive in our waters around early April but only come ashore at night. But it must be a dark night, overcast and no moonlight; they're so clumsy on land and easy prey for the larger gulls.'

We three sit there and listen intently to his words, supping our mugs of tea.

Mac asks: 'How many pairs nest on Bardsey?'

'It's difficult to be precise, but we think around 15,000 pairs, and each pair produces one chick,' replies the warden.[65] 'As you saw last night, they nest in burrows or in crevices in walls. We do know from our ringing records that the same pair come back to the same burrow every year. The parent birds leave in the autumn and split for the winter.'

Mac continues his questions. 'How do they find their way back?'

'If I'm honest,' says the warden, 'we don't really know. We think they navigate by the sun and stars, but have no hard proof.' He changes tack: 'Okay, lads, I have to get off to Nant and look at our mist nets up there.

---

65   A study in 2016 identified over 21,000 apparently occupied burrows, which represents a growth of over 5,000 birds since the previous census in 2008.

Have a good day's birding.' He quickly rinses his mug, grabs his bins and is off.

We manage our chores; I'm a dish washer and sweeper upper. We settle into our daily birding routines of morning patrols and counts, brief lunches and lazy afternoons watching and noting. The black notebook is always at hand. An occasional chase back to the obs at Christin to see a trapped rarity enlivens the day. The evening's cooked meal and subsequent roll call census forms the day's conclusion. We proudly add our sightings to the records.

At lights out we retire to our rooms and chatter for a few minutes, discussing the day's events. Thoughts are collected. Thoughts of just where we are, in this old schoolhouse on a remote island off the Welsh coast.

This is so different. It begins to sink in that our world has changed. Nature is closer now. In a very small way we are part of a bigger, wider world of natural science which exists beyond our tramps along the north Wirral shore.

Nature's calm, slow beauty is laid out here for all to see. I have a favourite spot to watch the ocean. At the north end, beyond the collection of cottages which is Nant, there's a field which slopes down to the rocky indents where the sea swells and crashes. There's a spread of wind-torn gorse bushes at the top of this field; home to two families of stonechats. On a warm afternoon with just a breeze, this spot does it for me. The colours. The quiet. The shining sea. Time to reflect on all those nature moments since I left the safety of that hospital bed.

Today the island is as splendid as it was when I first went there as a 15-year-old. I have been back three times in my late sixties: a day trip and two one-week stays. The journey over is not so scary now; life jackets are available, and the transport is a modern bright yellow, twin-engined modified lobster-fishing boat. The boat carries ten passengers and their gear, and the trip takes 25 minutes. Although the transportation is different, the job of boatmen to Bardsey has stayed in the Evans family. The new boatman is Colin, grandson to Farmer Wil. We reminisce about my first trip from the beach at Aberdaron.

On one of the visits I was keen to meet a Bardsey resident, a top bird photographer by the name of Ben Porter. I had seen many of his marvellous bird photographs in the Bardsey Obs daily blog. Ben has his own website, showcasing many of his remarkable shots. I wandered up to Cristin and asked if this guy Ben Porter, was on the island, as I would love to meet him and learn from his experience. I was 68 at the time and my passion for wildlife photography, a retirement project, was still in its infancy.

Steve Stansfield, the warden, said, 'Very sorry, he's off the island today as he's taking his GSCEs.'

It had never crossed my mind that Ben was still at school, for goodness' sake. It turned out that he was the charming 16-year-old son of the Porters, who were then farmers at Ty Pellaf.

Today, as a result of 50 years of ringing records, we know much more of the Manx shearwater's natural history. One bird, ringed on Bardsey in 1957 when it was thought to be five years old, was re-trapped in April 2002. This makes it the oldest ever recorded bird, 50 years of age. We also know that manxies spend the winter in the south Atlantic off the coast of Brazil. That's a journey of at least 10,000 kilometres. During its lifetime this bird will have clocked up a million kilometres in migration alone. Naturalists now know that shearwaters do not rely on stars to navigate, and there are no landmarks on the journey to help. Recent research has identified that shearwaters, like many other species, are able to sense, to read, the earth's magnetic field in order to navigate these featureless oceans. It is suggested this navigation aid is accomplished at the molecular level, with tiny crystals of magnetite in their eyes. There is strong evidence that the properties of quantum mechanics are at the heart of this navigational biology. Quite extraordinary.

It's early Saturday morning. Colin the boatman is picking me up later in the morning, taking our group of three senior birders back to the mainland in his yellow lobster boat-cum-ferry. It's time to leave Bardsey. As I'm older now, this might well be my last visit. The thought sits uncomfortably for a moment. I need to visit two special places.

The walk down the track to the plantation at Nant takes ten minutes at most. I'm drawn to that patch of steep meadow overlooking the ocean, where as a 15-year-old I would idle my afternoons beneath the stonechat's gorse amongst the manxies' burrows. The magic is still there. The sea breeze cools my face. I sit with arms clasped around my bent knees looking at the ocean. There is a reassuring rhythm to all this. Seasons. Migrations. There are warm greetings and there are sad farewells.

Count my breaths. Repeat a silent mantra. Clear the busy space. Difficult though that always is. Settle. Memories …

A weasel runs at full pelt along a hillside's sheep track, suddenly stops to look around, and then jumps a good 6 inches in the air for no apparent reason.

An osprey circles a lochan just after dawn, spots a trout and dives with its talons outstretched, ready for the kill.

A barn owl flaps silently by, following the path of a ditch, its magnificent round head peering into the reeds and long grass.

A robin singing for all its worth on a hawthorn branch.

Are these memories the gossamer wefts that nature weaves into the very essence of some lucky individuals?

There is time. I have an hour to spare before the crossing, and I tell my fellow passengers I'm going to climb the mountain again one last time.

'Do you want company?' I must have looked unsettled at the suggestion, as the enquirer quickly follows with, 'Or would you like some privacy?'

'If you don't mind,' I reply.

The walk from Cristin is the very same as the one I took on my first visit all those 53 years ago, but this time the pace is carefully considered, slower. Thoughts are on each move of my legs; every step up a conscious call. Physical action requires consideration. Not because it's a struggle. In that conscious moment there's reassurance in every move. I can still make it up this 'mountain'. I'm still in control of my bones. It feels good. Nature is still close and precious.

Present time stretches in a way I had not thought possible. All in good time. All in good time. Corrupting urgency is for younger men.

A soft northerly breeze cools. It will be here for a while yet. A skylark trills and black choughs play in the updrafts. They really are a delight to watch. The path zigzags through the moorland trinity of heather, bracken and gorse.

The last steps to this summit. To the south the lighthouse is bathed in fresh clear light. My eyes rest easy on this pleasant isle. (*Photo 38*)

A final sit-down with a flask of coffee and a buttered laverbread buttie, using up the remnants of my rations. Sea colours change and collide as light hides behind high, wispy cloud. A northern wheatear in black, silvery-grey and white livery sits nearby on a boulder covered in ancient lichen. The orange of the lichen patches matches the orangey-pink of the wheatear's throat feathers, ruffled by the breeze. Is he interested in my laverbread? I tear off a piece and throw it in his direction. His dark eyes inspect the morsel and then he looks at me. He decides I'm no threat. I'm part of his world and he's part of mine. His white tail feathers flash bright as he picks up a titbit and retreats to a safer distance. (*Photo 39*)

Visibility is good. Cardigan Bay stretches to the south. To the east the headland at Aberdaron looks closer today. The dangerous Bardsey Sound shows all the whirls and eddies as befits Bardsey's Welsh name, Ynys Enlli, 'island in the currents'.

A yacht with a single sail, a pale blue genoa, heads north in the direction of Anglesey, leaving an evanescent narrow wake. Dreams of Roy on his boat, *Sea Loone*.

A young peregrine from this year's brood passes by at eye level, touring the cliff face. We share the island. (*Outside back cover.*)

The mountain has not changed, but the uncomfortable isolation it once offered to a young man is now a memory.

'I'm all right, Ma.'

Colin's yellow lobster boat appears from behind the headland, across the Sound. He will be with us in 20 minutes to ferry me and a few other souls.

It's time I went.

'I'm ready when you are, Colin. I have a few pennies in my pocket,' I whisper to the wind. I can't help but think on: 'It's been some time since I nearly made that final crossing as a very sick ten-year-old'.

EPILOGUE: EVOLUTION AND
THE ENLIGHTENMENTS

Ever since my first conversation about evolution on Hilbre Island as a young teenager, a rudimentary knowledge of what it is and how it works has been a fixation. Having spent so much time with nature I continue to be surprised by the beauty and complexity of the world we live in. An understanding of how science works when reason and evidence triumph only adds to that sense of wonder.

Rigorous, reasoned knowledge is the peer-reviewed, layered and accumulated experimental results of insights of the time. The accumulated ken of those who have gone before. Incremental understanding normally builds slowly, but occasionally there comes along a Newton, an Einstein or a Darwin; current theories and ideas are thrown aside, and deep, original thinking creates a paradigm shift in our grasp of the fundamental principles of the world we inhabit. These seismic insights provide a new context for further research and yet more layered understanding, until the possibility, no matter how remote, of another paradigm shift comes along.

Charles Erasmus Darwin (1809–1882) heralded such a shift when he published a new biological theory of natural selection in 1859. Trained for ordination in the Anglican community, he was only too aware that his ideas differed fundamentally from the Church's strict doctrine of divine creation. Conflict was going to be inevitable.

The Church had plenty of form. Back in 1632, the brilliant Galileo published the results of his telescopic observations and calculations, confirming Copernicus's theory that our earth was not the centre of the universe. We were, like other planets, satellites of our sun. This went against the Church's doctrine, and eventually, 11 years later in 1633, Galileo was declared a heretic, albeit by a narrow ecclesiastical court majority. He had to recant, and was held under house arrest for the rest of his life. He was not allowed to publish again. He died in 1642. It took until 1992, 350 years after his death, for the Vatican to formally clear Galileo of any wrongdoing. It is interesting to note that Nicolas Copernicus (1473–1543), a Polish mathematician/cleric, was not hindered in his studies.

Darwin knew his theory would put him in serious conflict with the Christian church. Indeed, it is widely considered that this was the main reasons why it took over 15 years before he finally published his theory, long after he had come to his conclusions on evolution by natural selection. It was only the prospect of being pipped at the post by Alfred Russel Wallace that propelled him into the perils of publication.

We may think evolution is a modern idea, but it was first understood by several early Greek thinkers. Anaximander (610–546 BCE) from Miletus, now part of Turkey, on the Ionian coast, suggested that life originated in water and that simple forms preceded complex forms. That was over 2,600 years ago. Democritus, who we met in an early chapter, also thought that the simplest forms of life arose from a kind of primordial ooze.

Empedocles (c.490–430 BCE) lived in the port of Akragas (now Agrigento) in Sicily at the same time as Democritus. He is also mentioned by Aristotle, who pointed out that many animals were not always able to reproduce and it was only those able to survive through their inherited natural talents such as courage or speed, who did so.

In his remarkable life, Empedocles not only devised a theory of natural selection but also proposed that everything in existence is made of different combinations of the four elements: in his words, air, fire, wind and earth. These were the 'fourfold root of all things'. His statement, 'Nothing new comes or can come into being; the only change that can occur is a change in the arrangement of the elements', is the first inkling we have of the modern law that mass is conserved in chemical reactions.

According to Aristotle, Empedocles was the first to give light a finite speed. 'Empedocles says that the sun's light arrives first in the intervening space before it reaches our eyes or the earth. This seems reasonable.' He was also a vegetarian from a moral perspective; he believed human souls inhabit animal bodies, so it would be wrong to eat any animal.

Epicurus (341–270 BCE) was another who extolled a version of evolution; in a letter to Herodotus he explained that nature did not always get it right and had to learn lessons from experience.

Epicurus is a fascinating thinker. Today we tend to use the adjective 'epicurean' to describe a person who loves the good life and especially good food; but this is way off the mark. Epicurus certainly suggested that we need to sate our desires, but his thinking was not just about the pure hedonism of physical pleasure. He advocated living in a way which brought maximum satisfaction to both mind and body, but he specifically said this did not mean overindulgence, as this brought suffering. He discouraged activities which might feed the ego (lust for power or fame) and disturb an individual's virtue. Epicurus regarded ataraxia (a state of tranquillity due to freedom from fear) and aponia (absence of pain) as the height of happiness. To be even more specific, he was not too keen on passionate love and marriage: recreational sex was fine, but not necessary.

He taught in his 'garden', where anyone could attend – and, unusual for the time, this included women and slaves. His influences lasted well into our modern world, and several notable individuals claim to be Epicurean, including Thomas Jefferson, Denis Diderot and Christopher Hitchins. I would suggest that the ability to live humbly in nature, be part of nature, and see nature as life's greatest pleasure is an epicurean idea. We can live with nature and enjoy the world, bringing great pleasures to ourselves and to others when we are free from pain and anxiety.

The views on evolution, as espoused by Empedocles and Epicurus, were not shared by the Athenian, Plato (428–c.348 BCE) and his pupil Aristotle (384–322 BCE). Plato thought each species had a 'form' existing in another realm as a template of perfection. You can understand why early Christians adopted suitable parts of Plato's reasoning to support their teachings. Aristotle, Plato's student, went to great lengths to classify the entire living world, starting with plants and finally ending up with Man [sic]. In between were many individual 'forms', but these were thought to have been created independently.

Aristotle's analysis held sway for millennia, until the start of the Enlightenment in the 17th century brought its own questions and upheavals in many forms of thinking and scientific method. Why this long gap, nearly 2,000 years?

To set the scene it is worth looking at Greek religion at the time of the early philosophers. A pantheon of gods prevailed, who had all the exaggerated characteristics of the human condition. They represented the frailties, strengths and resilience of mere mortals. Early Greeks were also animistic, believing there were many sacred places such as rivers, forests, caves and mountains, so it was in those places that many of the most important religious rituals took place.

Greek philosophical schools, led by the likes of Plato's Academy and Aristotle's Lyceum, were still offering their services 600 years later, in the 4th century CE. But in 314 the Roman emperor Constantine converted to Christianity, giving it a huge plug. He was impressed by Christianity and, Rome still ruling Greece, it suited his political purposes to set up a new, and Christian, Rome in Constantinople. Many historians claim that in so doing he planted the seed for the demise of this rich lode of Greek philosophical thoughts and ideas.

How did Christians at the time, in the first centuries of the new millennium, understand their new religion? The important first principle was simply:

> There is only one God. He is all-knowing and all-powerful. There is no pantheon of gods. His Word and teachings, through Jesus, have been codified into the Bible, whose authority is not to be questioned. The Bible gives us all we need to know. Alterations and dilutions are not permitted.

Early western Christianity had no room for rational speculation; this view persisted well into Galileo's time. To this day we still see a similar attitude in several congregations, where reason gives way to a closed, literal adherence to scripture as the only true word of God. (This strict interpretation of old texts applies in many religions, of course, not just Christianity.)

According to early Christian scripture, God exists separately from nature. He created nature but is not part of it, and we surely need to praise him for nature's beauty. He is divine and not of this world. Early Christians believed it to be a heresy to worship nature. They argued that there were no holy places – only holy people, saints. If a particular location had a special religious significance it was because a holy person had been there, or someone had donated a saint's body part, or someone had had a holy vision.

It was just a matter of time before the early Christian administrators of the Greek state began to see the established schools of Greek philosophers as subversive, containing the seeds of heresy.

At the time of Augustine of Hippo (354–430 CE), Plato's ideas were well regarded in the Roman Empire. They had been structured into a form known as Neoplatonism by another eminent Greek philosopher, Plotinus (204–270 CE). Plato thought that man's [*sic*] body was an imperfect realisation of a 'perfect form' which only existed in a spiritual dimension beyond our knowledge. To a Christian, this perfect form looked very much like the soul. Plato considered body and soul to be quite different and distinct entities. Augustine used this differentiation to answer the vexed question 'Why does natural evil (earthquakes, disease, tsunami and so forth) exist if God is all-good, all-knowing and all-powerful?' Augustine suggested that God gave us free will and, in so doing, the choice between good and evil or the soul and the body. By attempting to nurture the soul we should keep our bodies pure. It is an interesting read to follow Augustine's logical attempt to justify disease, earthquakes and the other forms of 'natural evil' in a world where God is a benign, all-knowing, all-seeing divinity.

By the end of the 6th century there were only traces left of what had once been a dynamic and thriving period of reasoned philosophical debate. The last surviving school, if not the same building, Plato's Academy, kept going by the Neoplatonists, was finally closed by the Christian Emperor Justinian in 529 CE. It had lasted 875 years from Plato's death.

Most historians agree that by 476 CE the western Roman empire had ceased to function. Historians posit that it is not coincidental that the West receded into what we call the Dark Ages. Although the Renaissance came along in the 12th century in the form of fine architecture and other manifestations of visual art, it would be another 500 years before science and reason began to emerge from the shackles placed on rational speculation and empirical observation by the Christian Church. However, during the Dark Ages not all was lost to the enquiring mind. The search for knowledge continued in the East.

The Greeks' philosophical thought had long stimulated their Arab friends and neighbours. By the 8th century the cultural and scholarship nexus had shifted to Baghdad and other centres of Islamic learning, and the 8th to 13th centuries became known as the Golden Age in Arabic thinking. Muslim scholars at the time, such as Avicenna and Abu Bakr, were responsible for many remarkable advances in the way we think.

Abu Ali al-Husayn ibn Sina (Avicenna, 980–1037) is considered the most eminent of this group. He lived in what is now Iran, and wrote over 450 books. His medical tome was still the reference point in European medical thinking in 1650, and the original translations of his work influenced the European Enlightenment 600 years after his death. One of his assertions offers an insight into the man: he divided humanity into those who have either religion or wit, but rarely both.

Had it not been for the golden age of Arabic translations from those early Greek texts, the thoughts of Aristotle, Plato and other great Greek thinkers would not be available today. Arabic scholars and clerics did not see texts of science and reason as threats. They saw them as concomitant parts of understanding divinity. For Muslims at the time, science and especially mathematics, were God-given and unified with nature. Later, European scholars had the Arabic texts translated into Latin.

Here's just one example of mathematics in nature. It's called the Fibonacci sequence, and it's sort of cute. If you take the two numbers 0 and 1 (the number zero was introduced into algebra by Arabic thinkers in the late 8th century) and add them together you get a third number in the sequence, which is 1. If you then add the second and third number in the sequence you get the fourth number, 2. If you then add the third and fourth number, you get 3, and so on, each iteration adding the last two numbers to produce the next one. The sequence is 0, 1, 1, 2, 3, 5, 8, 13, 21, *ad infinitum*. This numerical sequence is be found everywhere in nature; flower buds, pinecones, vegetables, snail shells, and even in the human ear. The sequence was discovered in the early 11th century by an Italian by the name of Leonardo Pisano Bogollo, who lived in Pisa between 1170 and 1250. Fibonacci was his nickname, which roughly means 'son of Bonacci'. He also fervently advocated the use of the Arabic numeral system, the one we use today, over the old Roman numerical system of I, II, III, IV, V, VI, VII, VIII, IX, X etc.

Not only did algebra and trigonometry flourish in Persia to the east, but medicine benefited most from this cultural exchange between Ancient Greece and its Arabic neighbours.

Meanwhile, in Western Europe we were in what is known as our Middle Ages, which ran roughly from the 5th century to the 15th; it was the period which included the Crusades and the Inquisition. In historical terms the ideas of the Middle Ages were slowly overwhelmed by the ideas of what we now call the Enlightenment.

But before we move on to this time in our history I want to go back to our early Greek thinkers. Was not their time one of enlightenment? Did not our early Greek philosophers from 600 BCE onwards create a new view of the world, in which they moved on from the explanations of natural phenomena which were then embedded in the myths of a panoply of Gods with human personalities to a world where reason prevailed? For those philosophers, storms were now entirely natural events and not caused by an upset Poseidon. Lightning and thunder were taken away from Zeus's anger and given a reasoned explanation. The Greek city of Miletus is considered by many as the birthplace of Greek philosophy and therefore of Western thought as well. It is perhaps no coincidence that this revolution in thinking happened at a place and time where trade flourished between three different civilisations, namely Egypt, Mesopotamia and Greek Anatolia, so the city's culture was able to absorb ideas from North Africa and the Middle East.

So it was a second Enlightenment that was the sprawling intellectual, philosophical, cultural and social movement which spread through the United Kingdom, France, Germany and other parts of Europe during the 1700s. Enabled principally by the scientific revolution of the likes of Newton but also characterised by significant changes in philosophical thinking. The Enlightenment represented about as big a departure as possible from the Middle Ages.

David Hume (1711–1776) is high on the list of the philosopher's philosopher, and his thinking gave added weight to the development of natural sciences. He rigorously questioned the established religious views of his time. There is much to admire of Hume, but perhaps this well-known quote, the closing lines of his first enquiry, sums it up:

If we take in our hand any volume of divinity or school metaphysics …
let us ask, Does it contain any abstract reasoning concerning quantity or
number? No. Does it contain any experimental reasoning concerning
matter of fact and existence? No. Commit it then to the flames: for it
can contain nothing but sophistry and illusion.

David Hume's influence on that second Enlightenment is massive. He
is seen as the first philosopher in what has been called the early modern
period, to question the notion of divine reason. His predecessors such as
Descartes and Locke offered their analysis of how divine reason co-exists
with the great strides in science offered by the likes of Galileo Galilei and
Isaac Newton. Hume, however, took a step back and questioned the very
idea of a divine entity.

A major thinker in the later stages of this second Enlightenment
was Charles Darwin. When he published his On the Origin of Species
in November 1859, he magnanimously saluted the early Greek natural
philosopher Empedocles for 'shadowing forth the principle of natural
selection'.

The prevailing natural science orthodoxy of Darwin's day had both
scientific and religious strands co-existing easily. The science of nature
was predominantly one of classifying species, started by Aristotle but
developed significantly further in his many books by the Swede Carolus
Linnaeus (1708–1778). To Linnaeus, God was a given. His work describes
in detail God's creatures, and develops groups or classifications showing
where species have similarities. This is what we call taxonomy. A family
of creatures can have several genera, and a single genus can have
several species. A species can have several sub-species. This pyramidal
arrangement is driven predominantly by similarities in skeletons and, in
the case of birds, plumage. This taxonomy also includes plants and trees.

For 200 years before the time of Darwin's early work there had been
ideas concerning how animals evolve, despite the overbearing Christian
dogma that every form of life was created by God. When Darwin left
on his Beagle trip in 1833, it was believed that evolution worked by way
of offspring inheriting a parent's acquired characteristics. Jean-Baptiste
Lamarck (1744–1829) did not invent the idea of the inheritance of acquired
characteristics, but he did write about it in 1809. He suggested that when

a species uses parts of its body in a different way, such that physical body changes took place, then it was possible to pass on any changes to that individual's offspring. He suggested, for instance, that a heron's long legs came about as individual birds stretched their legs for their body feathers to remain dry, and this change was passed on. Similarly, giraffes evolved long necks simply by stretching when eating leaves off tall trees and then passing on the bodily result of all that stretching. This idea had traction amongst scientists at the time, but that seems strange to us now. There are so many examples where this type of inheritance does not prevail. A weightlifter trains and builds up body strength but this is not passed on to his children. An athlete who can run a mile in record time does not pass on that ability to her children. Miners who develop emphysema do not pass on the condition to their offspring. In each of these cases the parents may pass on a genetic predisposition towards the condition, but not the condition itself.

Darwin's breakthrough came when he proposed that evolution is a biological phenomenon where random changes in a species' biology offered different chances for the longer-term survival of that species by the further inheritance of that biological mutation. If these changes or mutations increase the chances for the members of that species to survive and thrive long enough to reproduce, then these biological changes will be passed on to a growing cohort of individuals. If these changes decrease the chances of survival, then they will less likely to live long enough to pass down these changes to subsequent generations.

Imagine if the first early Greek enlightenment had been allowed an unfettered blossoming of all the original thinking of Democritus, Empedocles and Epicurus up until the time of Darwin and Newton. Who knows what our intellectual landscape would look like now if those Greek schools of philosophy had not been closed?

Were these 1,000 years wasted?

There are many religious fundamentalists who suggest that Darwin's theory of evolution is just a theory and that it has equal standing with their creation theory. They are both theories after all, is their call. The moot point here is what do we mean exactly by the term 'theory'?

It can be taken to mean simply 'an unproven idea'.

Or not. Imagine a linear continuum, left to right, going from hunch to hypothesis, then to theory and finally to fact. Let's start on the left-hand side with a hunch. A hunch is an attempt by the scientific community to explain how an unexpected experimental result might be explained.

Experiments are designed, and other data is collected to see if a particular explanation has merit. For the hunch to survive there must be further independent, observable and repeatable results which support the proposition. As confidence grows, academics supporting the hunch are prepared to stick their necks out and call the original hunch a hypothesis (moving further right on our continuum). More evidence is collected to support the hypothesis, and further experiments are fashioned, particularly to *dis*prove the hypothesis. Next, without evidence having been found to disprove the hypothesis, especially from peer groups, there comes a time when the scientific community decide to put forward the hypothesis as a theory. This is a crucial moment.

Yet more experiments are devised to confirm the theory, often with competing academic bodies and by peer groups repeating crucial experiments. It is important that there are also experiments which try to disprove the theory. Eventually there comes a time when the academic community agrees that by and large the likelihood of the theory's being acceptable is so overwhelming that withholding assent to it would appear perverse.

This is a more formal occasion, when theory is recognised as fact. If one is a purist on these matters, then one can never be sure whether or not one day, perhaps in the far future, contrary evidence will come to light. But as time goes on, and yet more and more evidence comes along to support the fact, then this purist, philosophical point takes on the mantle of irrelevance.

So a theory, to the scientific community, is a 'well documented explanation'.

Which means that in 'creation theory' the word 'theory' means one thing, but in 'theory of evolution' it means something totally different. So there can be no comparison, no parallel drawn.

Getting back to Darwin, his theory is how evolution works, i.e. by natural selection. Although he did not have access to the mechanics to explain his theory, we now know that natural selection occurs by random gene mutation – errors – at the time of conception, when genes from both parents are replicated in every cell in the embryo.

It is thought that in the human embryo there are typically at least 60 such errors or mutations each time parents pass on their genes to their children. Sixty errors or mutations sounds like a lot, but as there are a total of 100 million DNA letters to be replicated the error rate is only 0.00006 per cent. This error rate has surprised the scientists who had thought there might be in the region of 100 or more errors; it suggests that human evolution is slower than originally predicted. The DNA letters are A, C, G and T, representing the four nucleotide bases of a DNA strand — adenine, cytosine, guanine, thymine.

Evolution has come a long way from the time when the theory of evolution was posited mainly on fossil record identification. Today significant branches of modern biochemistry, embryology and molecular biology confirm evolution. The code used to translate nucleotide sequences into amino acid sequences is essentially the same in all organisms. Moreover, the proteins in all organisms are invariably composed of the same set of 20 amino acids. This unity of composition and function is a powerful argument in favour of the common descent of even the most diverse organisms.

We are now at the point where all non-religious, academic scientific bodies around the world hold evolution to be fact. Creationists, however, openly question evolution, and they freely admit that their starting point is that God created us. If you start with such a premise it's difficult, some would say impossible, to debate the topic.

And where does religion to this day stand on evolution? The fundamentalists of the three main monotheistic religions prefer to ignore empirical, factual evidence, and still talk of creation theory as if it had weight equal to Darwin's theory. But within each discipline there are also, of course, many nuances and shades of belief.

It is thought less than 5 per cent of the UK population believe in divine creation. In the US, Gallup released its poll figures conducted there in 2017 on Creation Theory: 38 per cent of its respondents said they believed that God created man in our present form (down from 43 per cent ten years earlier), and the same percentage said they believed that humans evolved but God guided the process. According to Gallup only 24 per cent of Americans believe in evolution without divine guidance. Unsurprisingly, it is the less-educated Americans that are more likely to believe in creationism.

One of the preconditions for what often appears as human arrogance towards the environment is that too many of us still think we stand apart from other animals. For example, 38 per cent of Americans say they do not believe we have evolved from apes – they prefer to believe the Divine Creation story. But the scientific evidence that we have evolved from apes is irrefutable. Evolution is considered as fact by people with adequate critical thinking skills.

The trouble is, our world still pays unwarranted attention to those blinkered fundamentalists of whichever of the three Abrahamic faiths you take, who believe in Creation, where God stands outside nature, He designed nature and He looks on. People with such unenlightened views must find it very difficult to conclude that we are part of nature.

But truly being part of nature means we need to understand that a horsefly, a frog, a chimpanzee, a blue whale and a human are of equal value in the grand scheme of things.

Enlightenment, my trusted friend, where are you? We need you *now* more than ever.